Praise for *The (*

"[A] sexy 48-hour g
rediscover the magi
-*The Sunday New York Post*

"How long has it been since you and your partner showered together, made love in a new position, or lingered in bed all morning? If you can't recall, check out *The Great Sex Weekend.*"
-*Glamour*

"What a delicious idea. Rip the list of weekend chores off the refrigerator. Let the grass go un-mowed. Throw this book into your overnight bag, and along with some of the recommended toys, and go. *The Great Sex Weekend* reclaims time, creating a field of dreams for lovers. Take the *Weekend*, and your love life will benefit for years to come. Become a weekend warrior- for love."
-JAMES R. PETERSON, *Playboy*

"This book is like battery cables. Everyone should have it handy to jump start their love life!"

"A cornucopia of fun-filled yet practical ways to revitalize and add passion to any sexual relationship."
-LONNIE BARBACK, Ph.D., author of *For Yourself: The Fulfillment of Female Sexuality*, and *For Each Other*

"After two kids and ten years of marriage, we'd slipped into a sexual rut. The book gave us incentive to break our pattern. Now we're closer and more open to fun in bed than before."

"The authors...cover everything in terms of preparing for the lollapalooza getaway, from how to really make romantic moves to suggesting cozy lodgings in a handful of major cities."
-*New York Newsday*

The Great Sex Weekend forced us to pay attention to each other, which is something we were both hungry for, and didn't even know.

"Helps Rekindle the sparks"
-*American Woman*

GETAWAY GUIDE TO THE GREAT SEX WEEKEND

A PROVEN PROGRAM BY NATIONAL EXPERTS

PEPPER SCHWARTZ, PH.D.

and JANET LEVER, PH.D.

WORLDWIDE ROMANCE PUBLICATIONS
Seattle, WA and Los Angeles, CA
ISBN: 978-0-9855210-0-4

Portions of this book were previously published in *The Great Sex Weekend: A 48-Hour Guide to Rekindling Sparks for Bold, Busy or Bored Lovers* by G. P. Putnam's Sons

Book design by Jessica J. Young
Interior illustrations by Ansley Pearce
Cover design and art by Ansley Pearce

Photo of Pepper Schwartz by Ingrid Pope Sheldon for *Seattle Woman Magazine*; Photo of Janet Lever by Brian Joseph Gillespie

Library of Congress Control Number 2012938121
Getaway Guide to the Great Sex Weekend
1. Sex in marriage. 2. Sex instruction.   3. Couples—Sexual behavior. 4. Romantic Travel.

To our Road-testers,
for helping us create the weekend.

CONTENTS

APPENDICES

INTRODUCTION

Why Most Couples Need This Book
(And How to Persuade a Reluctant Partner to Get with the Program)

This book can jump-start your sex life in a single weekend. After a career researching sex, we can assure you that most couples who have been together a year or longer need this program. After the initial days and nights of your relationship when you couldn't keep your hands off each other, everyday life takes over. It is a documented fact: For the majority of couples, even after a short period of time, the frequency of lovemaking decreases dramatically.

If you're in the lucky 20 percent who are as sexually active or passionate as you ever were, this book can help you sustain your fabulous sex life. We know your THREE secrets, based on our own surveys: (1) good sexual communication, that includes building anticipation about a "date night" or upcoming leisurely weekend morning; (2) a willingness to try new things (e.g. positions or toys) to ward off stale routines; and (3) most important, taking the time to set the right mood for romance.

This book is organized around this knowledge. We know we can help the vast majority of couples, who are not bold sexual adventurers, to create an opportunity to try something new and feel the delight of renewed intimacy. It's so common for couples who work hard and have a busy social calendar to let another weekend slip by when they don't make love again. Chores, errands, kids' activities, job-related homework—those things all get done, yet when you think about it, you realize it's been two weeks since you had sex.

Or maybe you do make time to be together, and after a little bit of kissing, you have sex in the predictable, pleasant, but not wholly passionate way that has become part of your intimate life together.

Why don't people have more frequent and inventive sex? In short, they are either busy or bored--or both. Busy people may literally have to schedule sex, but sometimes they don't schedule it often enough, or worse yet, they break their own appointments. A couple's sex life suffers not because they don't love each other or know basic sexual techniques, but because sex always gets put on the back burner. The fast pace of everyday life, especially for people with children, makes it hard for even the most loving couples to have the kind of sex they'd like to have. If couples work different shifts or work weekends and/or nights—or just have an intense life—many weeks can go by before they can find time to make love.

Of course, being busy isn't the only reason for a neglected sex life. Long-term sexual relationships become routine. Each partner knows the other's body so well that they could find each other in a pitch-black room full of a hundred other naked bodies. Over the years, couples get into the habit of making love in exactly the same way. The sex can be satisfying, but often is boring. We all need innovation or surprise—and some permission to experiment—to keep things exciting.

If you think you're good at the basics of sex, but your sexual repertoire isn't as varied as you'd like, rest assured that you are like most Americans. Studies suggest that the range of adult sex play is fairly limited. One national survey found, for example, that just over a third of all couples have taken a shower together. Another study found that just under a third of all couples ever make a "date night" to help keep the romance alive. Just over a quarter have ever used a sex toy together. Perhaps the saddest statistic of all: Less than a quarter of couples even dimmed the lights or turned off the TV during their lovemaking.

Data from a respected study conducted at the University of Chicago show that even though the vast majority of Americans have experienced oral sex, it is only occasionally included during lovemaking. The same study showed, however, that many Americans find a wide range of sexual activities appealing, even if they haven't found a way to move them from fantasy into their real sex life.

WHY THIS GUIDE WORKS

The program on which you are about to embark has been tested and works. It was tried on dozens of willing volunteers whom we call our "road-test couples." These included married and cohabiting couples, ranging in age from their twenties to their fifties. Most are heterosexual; a few are same-sex couples. This program worked for both. After following the weekend program, each couple filled out an extensive questionnaire with comments and criticism. Some of their suggestions improved on our original ideas. We quote some of their commentary and tips throughout the book so you can read how other people experienced the weekend program.

We are both professors of sociology who have studied sexuality and intimate relationships for nearly forty years. Both of us teach university courses in human sexuality. Pepper Schwartz is a past president of the Society for the Scientific Study of Sexualities and is currently the Chief Relationships Expert for PerfectMatch.com.

And we have both worked on major surveys probing people's most private sexual behaviors and attitudes. Results from one study—based on in-depth interviews and questionnaires from 12,000 people—were published in Pepper's book (with Philip Blumstein), *American Couples.* After leading teams of researchers that designed the three largest magazine sex surveys ever tabulated, Janet has been the senior analyst on annual internet sex surveys that are a joint venture between *ELLE* magazine and msnbc.com; these are among the largest surveys on various sex topics to date.

We publish in popular media as well as academic journals. For all of the 1990s, we coauthored *Glamour* magazine's "Sex and Health" column. In addition to answering readers' questions, every month we asked questions of our readers. Their thousands of letters have helped us understand what people want to know and what has helped some of them create an exciting sex life.

In the course of our professional careers, we have used the work of academicians and clinicians in many disciplines. We have picked from the best social science studies, therapeutic models, and other experts' advice to formulate this program.

We've put into this book a lifetime of knowledge and interest in making people's sex lives better. We are confident that you will have the same response as our road-test couples—when you return from your weekend getaway, you'll be happier and feel closer. As one road-tester wrote after his weekend:

> *My wife is my number-one priority in life, but I rarely act like it! I tend to get caught up in my work, and that steals time from our relationship. But this weekend I was able to consciously make her my number-one focus, and it was wonderful!*

HOW THIS BOOK CAN HELP YOU

This book will help you revitalize your sexual and romantic life. We're not just recommending sex in new positions or new places at strange times. Even bold lovers can experience exciting sexual moments that, nevertheless, fail to create intimacy. Building a better sexual partnership requires expanding the emotional connection as well as sexual technique. Our book provides everything couples need for a fast weekend tune-up that really improves their sexual relationship.

This program will help you to create an easy, fun weekend project if you and your partner still have good feelings toward each other but have slipped into bad habits. *The Great Sex Weekend* provides an occasion to take a short time-out from everyday life and lavish attention on each other. Give us just a few days and well help you recapture the desire and playfulness that characterized the early days when you first fell in love.

Just as your car needs to be tuned periodically, every relationship needs to be recharged now and then. Your relationship needs tune-ups that not only keep it going but keep it humming. Think of our play-by-play guide as a handy manual to use again and again to maintain a higher level of sexual desire and satisfaction. When things drift back to where they were before you first tried this program, you'll know what to do. We present more options than you can fit into a single weekend, so there are plenty of ideas and variations for future weekend refreshers.

We expect that you'll return to this book and plan more sexy getaways, because they are fun, and because you are ready to try new ideas. Since readers have different comfort levels with sexual experimentation, we present options ranging from basic to intermediate to exotic. We encourage couples to discuss which ideas are appealing, which might be appealing sometime in the future, and which ideas make one or both partners feel uncomfortable. *Nothing is mandatory.* Every individual's comfort zone differs and must be respected at all times.

A few parts of the program are highly recommended because they provide the basic foundation for a creative sex life, but most parts are optional. We invite you to customize the program to your own tastes, but don't be surprised if some of our more exotic suggestions look more enticing the next time you plan a "Great Sex Weekend."

This book is not meant for people with serious sexual problems. Although our program can be helpful for re-motivating a partner with low sexual desire, couples whose sexual problems seem bigger than that should seek a good sex therapist. If you need help finding a therapist, ask your doctor or your local family-planning clinic for a referral. You also can visit the website of the American Association of Sex Educators, Counselors and Therapists (www.aasect.org) and click on "Locate a Professional" to see a list of the nationally certified sex therapists and counselors in your state.

If you're in a troubled relationship, we suggest you wait until things are better before you attempt the weekend program. Couples who are trying to sort out serious problems don't need the extra pressure. The exercises we suggest require goodwill and trust. If the idea of this weekend makes either partner anxious, put it off until it feels right.

How to Get a Reluctant Partner to Participate

What if only one partner in the couple thinks the sexual relationship needs to be a few degrees hotter, or if only one of you thinks it's possible to take this much time off to tinker with your sex life? *If your partner is a workaholic and likes the idea but hesitates to schedule a time, suggest the shorter program outlined in "A 24-Hour Plan" at the back of this book.*

Plan a date far enough in advance that it is almost impossible for your partner to refuse. If your partner claims not to be able to give up even a single day, it's justifiable to say that your relationship not only deserves this time but that you really want it. When your partner minimizes *the need* for this program, your task becomes more challenging. Here are a few ideas for convincing a reluctant partner:

1. *Give this book to your partner as a gift that holds the promise of intimacy and pleasure.* Treat the idea in a lighthearted manner instead of gravely announcing, "We've got to do something about our sex life!" Offer the program as a romp. If it doesn't live up to its full promise, at a minimum you'll have a great weekend together.

2. *Promote the idea of a sexy getaway as an adventure—something that will require a little reach for both of you.* Think of a weekend spent improving your sex life as you might think of signing up for a weekend golf clinic. It's not that you're bad at golf; you go to be even better at something you really enjoy.

3. *If your partner is good-natured but lazy, offer to take care of planning the entire weekend.* Book an over-night trip to a mystery location. All he or she has to do is show up. Your time making thoughtful arrangements will be seen as a gift. Once you pull it off your partner may be more inclined to help make the next one happen.

A few final thoughts on this topic:

Don't pressure your partner—introduce the idea and give him or her time to ponder it. Your partner will probably get over any initial resistance and eventually become intrigued with the idea.

But do persevere. If you don't take this kind of time to nurture your sexual relationship, there's a big price to pay. Besides losing the excitement that good sex provides, over time couples can experience erosion of intimacy and confidence in their personal desirability.

With a little time and less effort than you think, you can fix or avoid these problems.

Remember: the more options you explore, the more likely you are to find new things you both enjoy. In one of our recent surveys we learned that about half of Americans buy books like this one—but not even half of those who read sex self-help books or magazine articles ever actually try out the suggestions.

Those who do put ideas into practice agree that they work like a charm, and were very beneficial to their relationships.   So….don't just read this book, give it your own road test, and let us know if you like our program. Visit *www.thegreatsexweekend.com* to share your experiences, or to get ideas from other people's weekend highlights. See our featured destinations there, and also on *www.hisandhersvacations.com*

Many of you, we are sure, will end up agreeing with this road-tester's testimonial:

> *We needed something like this to remind us of how important we are to each other. Life has a way of distracting you and making you look elsewhere. This program forced us to pay attention to one another, which is something we were both hungry for and didn't even know it.*

CHAPTER ONE

Planning the Setting: Time, Place, and Mood

Our weekend began as soon as we started reading the book! We got so turned on, we started planning our weekend immediately. My husband left work early three times during the week we were planning our trip so we could make love before the kids got home from school This was truly unusual; he's an executive who always works until at least seven o'clock.

Follow the play-by-play suggestions in this book, and at the very least you'll have a really romantic, erotic, fulfilling weekend. We know you'll have fun, but we're optimistic that this book will do more: You will likely build a higher level of desire, exploration, and satisfaction into your sex life by following the guided program.

We provide a lot of new ideas for sex innovations and surprises, but you make the weekend your own by taking what you want to customize a sexy romp that suits your own tastes and schedule. Everything we recommend is safe, so it's simply a matter of what appeals to you and your partner, and what you agree to actually try.

Before you begin the weekend program, we strongly recommend that both you and your partner read this book to see what's ahead and what you'll need. We hope that each partner will participate in the planning and preparations.

We both took responsibility. We were equally excited about "the project."

There are exceptions to this rule. If one partner wants to orchestrate the whole weekend to surprise a willing partner by giving the book and sex getaway as a gift, it can work with the inspired partner doing all the planning.

My husband whisked me off without telling me where we were going. It was one of the most romantic things he ever did.

I was glad my husband hadn't read the book. He had no idea what was coming and was delighted by surprise after surprise.

SCHEDULING THE TIME

Assuming that both of you are designing this Great Sex Weekend, first you need to agree on a date—maybe a backup date, too—so this *really will* happen. At least, pick a date by which you promise each other you will make a reservation to get away or set a time for an at-home weekend.

We strongly urge you to devote an entire weekend to the program. If you can manage to dedicate only one day, choose a weekend when you can add on a luxurious Sunday morning. Road-testers were creative in adapting our suggestions to fit their work schedules

and budgets. Some road testers combined the getaway
with the celebration of a special occasion, like a
birthday or anniversary.

It is certainly possible to have a Great Sex
Weekend at home, too. If that appeals to you, you'll
find a whole appendix on the "At Home Option" at the
end of this book devoted to suggestions for preparing,
even transforming, your home to create an especially
romantic and private setting.

GETTING AWAY FROM HOME

> *We went to a hotel in Vegas because they*
> *have things you don't get at home or in an*
> *ordinary hotel, like mirrors above and beside*
> *the bed, dimmer lights everywhere, and an*
> *extra-large bathtub.*

If you can, we advise you to go away for the
weekend. Your house is full of reminders of things you
need to do and other distractions.

Selecting the right getaway location and making
reservations is important. Pick a setting that appeals
to you both. If she hates rustic places, don't take her to
one; if he hates pretentious resorts where everyone is
dressed up, find some middle ground. Here are the
things you should look for:

The location should be easy to get to. It's a bad
idea to start the weekend with any hassle. If a short
hop on a shuttle plane takes you someplace romantic,
fine, but these days getting in and out of most airports is
such an energy drain that it detracts from time that
could be better spent enjoying the program. In major
cities where traffic snarls make driving out of town
unpredictable, consider checking into a nice downtown

hotel where the service is great and the atmosphere is glamorous. And we always give extra points to resorts that feature a great spa for your relaxation and enjoyment. A getaway can be geographically close to home, yet totally out of the ordinary.

QUICK TIP #1: If you're going by car, you might consider renting something that's especially fun or outrageous, like a classic car, convertible, jeep, or sports car.

QUICK TIP #2: Some places may sound romantic but aren't. If you have a friend with a cabin in the woods, be cautious to be sure it has the amenities you need. Get some information before committing. Nice, clean cabins with all the modern conveniences in beautiful settings can be perfect sites for your weekend.

QUICK TIP #3: In general, we don't recommend bed-and-breakfasts. They can be charming, but most don't offer nearly enough privacy. Consider only those that provide detached cottages, or rooms with thick walls and private bathrooms.

QUICK TIP #4: Create your own checklist of what you want in a hotel, then be sure your hotel has enough of those features before you book it. Here are some features you may want to consider:

- Both a shower and a bathtub. If bathing together holds appeal, ask if they have any rooms with oversize tubs (extra points for a Jacuzzi).

- Room service.
- Bar refrigerators are a plus. (You can always bring a cooler if the hotel offers everything else you want.)
- Adult movies on pay-per-view or a dvd player (so you can bring along your own erotica, if that appeals to you both).
- Queen-size bed (extra points for a king-size or canopy bed).
- Charm. Seek a place with out-of-the-ordinary rooms or nice views. (Extra points for a balcony or fireplace.)

QUICK TIP #5: Every hotel has some small, dark, or noisy rooms. These days you can book a hotel that offers an online tour of the premises, including the guest rooms (sometimes, you can see the exact room you're booking). You can always tell the reservation clerk that this is to be a special weekend, and to please hold one of the better rooms for you.

> *Tell your readers to ask for a room away from the elevator; we didn't, and the noise detracted from an otherwise perfect weekend.*

> *We always request a room adjacent to a stairwell or an end unit; that guarantees privacy on at least one side of the suite.*

> *I wish I'd asked whether any conventions were going on that weekend. There was one, which made the hotel crowded and detracted from our romantic mood.*

QUICK TIP #6: Guard your privacy. It is essential to feel that neither your mood nor your activities will be interrupted. Create a policy about cell phones, blackberries, time on the ipad, or anything else your partner finds an annoying intrusion on private time. Agree on how often or when you'll call to check on the kids, pets, work, etc.

At the back of this book, in the appendix called "Getaway Places" you will find a selected list of romantic places to stay in or near a few dozen locales in the United States and Canada. There we also describe a few close-by amazing international destinations for those lucky enough to have the extra time and resources for a Great Sex Splurge. Check out our website: **www.thegreatsexweekend.com** for featured destinations.

OPTIONAL LONGER-TERM PREPARATIONS

Do I need to diet first? No, don't put off the weekend because you're waiting to reach your "best weight." We live in a culture that idolizes slim, athletic bodies. The challenge for both women and men is to feel desirable even if they aren't at their ideal weight. The slow, sensuous approach toward lovemaking that we suggest makes people feel sexy and turned on. Our motto: If You Think Sexy and Act Sexy, You Will Be Sexy.

If you feel self-conscious about your body, there are things you can do to feel more attractive and comfortable. The low, soft light we recommend not only sets the mood but is flattering. Candles provide the most "generous" lighting effect. We recommend that women who are embarrassed about their extra body weight undress in the bathroom and emerge in a silky, loose-fitting garment (like a dressing gown, short kimono, or oversize man's-style shirt).

QUICK TIP #7: *If it's fun for you to do some online shopping together, you can order some new, sexy clothes or lingerie (See Appendix 4).* We're quite sure that your current wardrobe has everything you need for a sexy getaway. However, buying something new can add to the anticipation of the weekend. Feeling well dressed, especially if your partner is the kind to notice and compliment you on how you look, can make you feel extra sexy.

> *He loves seeing me in sexy lingerie. As a present to him, I bought stockings and a light-blue garter belt with matching bra for me to wear. I had them gift-wrapped and had him open this gift right before dinner Friday night. He couldn't wait to get home.*

We hasten to add that it is not only men who get aroused by sexy underwear or great new clothes. Victoria's Secret also sells men's sexy silk boxers, bikini underwear, and kimonos. A woman loves to see her man dressing just for her, but he may soon appreciate how these garments make him feel sexy and attractive, too.

16

*My husband is a jeans kind of guy. He really
surprised me by bringing a beautiful suit and
tie for our Saturday dinner out. I was flattered
that he wanted to look good for me. That was
a real turn-on.*

QUICK TIP #8: Think creatively about the clothes that
are already in your wardrobe. Many women already
have teddies or sheer camisoles, and use them
strictly as underwear. In the spirit of this weekend, be
more adventurous than usual. Wear your teddy under a
blazer or suit top instead of a blouse. One of our road-
testers suggested another variation on the lingerie
theme, proving yet again that the power of suggestion
should never be underestimated:

*During dinner I told my husband that I wasn't
wearing any panties under my dress. He rushed
through our dinner to get back to our hotel for
an evening of passionate lovemaking.*

SUGGESTED SHORT-TERM PREPARATIONS

Weeklong Abstinence

*The minute we made sex off-limits, we were
dying for it.*

Most people don't need this tip: If you have a
frequent sex life and want to enhance this getaway,
consider having a period of abstinence before you leave
for your weekend. You wouldn't want to eat a heavy
lunch if you knew a sumptuous banquet awaited you
that evening. Abstaining for the week before your sexy
getaway will heighten your appetite for sexual
extravagance.

Our road-test couples confirmed the old axiom that we always want what we can't have.

> *The abstinence worked for us. We were really hungry for each other by the time the weekend began.*

> *This was the first time we had to "repress" our desires since the hot, hormonal days of high school.*

Another reason for weeklong abstinence has its roots in the therapy program for couples developed by sex researchers Masters and Johnson. Abstaining from genital play shifts the emphasis away from goal-oriented (that is, orgasm-oriented) sexuality to sensuality. You can touch and caress each other. When you and your partner want close contact and want to get beyond cuddling, take turns massaging each other, avoiding the breasts and genitals. Gently knead the little tension knots on your partner's neck, feet, or hands, or massage the head. Very slowly give long strokes down the back, arms, and legs.

Notice how touching your partner gives you pleasure, too. Ask your partner to tell you what feels good and what does not. This simple exercise provides a good introduction to learning more about your own body and your partner's body in the week before you embark on the program. Touching all over the body reminds us that we have many erogenous zones besides the obvious ones. Getting aroused during the massage is understandable. But a little frustration is going to help create longing and anticipation that serve as a reminder of how much you really desire your partner's touch.

We added one more rule: We both swore we wouldn't play with ourselves as a way to make the anticipation that much sweeter. I think he held to his end of the bargain. I know I did, and it made me very excited.

QUICK TIP #9: Experiment with more verbal foreplay than usual. We know a sex counselor who tells men that if they start verbal foreplay in the morning, their partners will be begging them to have sex that night. The busier your day (hers or his), the more your partner appreciates that he or she is on your mind.

Verbal foreplay should be expressed in your own words. Say only what you mean and say it in a way that fits your style. Here are some suggestions from our road testers that might just get you thinking:

I called my fiancé Friday morning and said, "I can't wait until we start our sex getaway tonight." Then I dropped a hint that I had bought a new toy for us to play with that she'd never tried before.

For a few days before we went on our weekend, I left suggestive little messages on his private voice mail. He loved it.

My husband called me Friday afternoon, just before our "weekend" was to start, and told me what he was going to do to me—using the present tense, as if it were happening now.

If you prefer the written word, then text, email, or drop a handwritten note in a briefcase, or in the cupboard in front of the coffee cups, or taped to the toothpaste!

My husband sent an out-of-character romantic letter signed "See you tonight—Your Secret Admirer."

I knew I'd try to overcome my resistance to oral sex when my lover sent me a steamy note that read: "Deep pools of viscous you—I long to go there."

Several women have described "treasure hunts" in which they are the "treasure." One left her lover a note at the front door that led to a pitcher of margaritas, where another sexy note yielded his next clue, and so on, until he reached the "treasure"—his provocatively dressed wife.

I used an old lipstick to write a countdown on our bedroom mirror the entire week before. He was really excited by the time it read "Just 1 more day."

COMMUNICATING EXPECTATIONS

Our road-testers unanimously reported that seeing the possibilities spelled out ahead of time was enticing and, for many, titillating. Some of those couples had already tried many of the activities we describe, although they confessed they hadn't done some of these things in a long time. Some knew their partner would be "up for anything," but other road-testers weren't sure of their partners' reactions about new sexual activities and didn't feel comfortable just coming out and asking for what they wanted. Some were also feeling a little concerned that their partners might want to try an exercise that they themselves were not ready for.

The best way to reduce pressure and avoid disappointment is to keep an open mind: *Don't expect to do everything we suggest on a single getaway weekend.* This guide is designed to be used over and over. For couples who are open to experimentation, there are ample suggestions for how to turn up the heat the next time around.

Several road-testers found discussing sexual interests to be kind of awkward. They felt that they needed help making intimate requests. Happily, a few couples came up with some natural and easy solutions. Our nod goes to the partners who each read the book and highlighted in different colors those exercises and activities that interested them the most. Some even put stars or asterisks in the margins when something really piqued their interest.

> *We each reviewed what we had highlighted. Knowing what the other person wanted got us both excited about the coming adventure.*

> *He only skimmed the book. I read it word for word, so in the car on the way down to the hotel we talked about what I wanted to try. It made our commute fun, and he enthusiastically supported my choices.*

CHAPTER TWO

Thinking Ahead: What to Take

We had fun shopping for a new bra for the occasion. With both of us in the dressing room "voting" on the best choice, it was a great precursor to a sensual weekend.

In this chapter we suggest you purchase specific items that will enhance your experience. We've done the planning and legwork so that you can devote your own creative energies to the fun parts of this weekend getaway. Most of these items are easily available online (see our Appendix 4) or in stores at the mall.

We make lots of suggestions here for you to choose whatever appeals to you. Nothing in this book is required. Shopping together, whether online or in a store, can be a lot of fun for you, and shows your willingness to create a truly special time for sex and love. But if you can't gather these things ahead of time, shopping at the start of your weekend is not a bad choice. One road-tester adamantly drove home this point:

I was too busy to prep—and being too busy is why we needed the weekend in the first place! 1 relieved my feelings of guilt by suggesting that we shop Saturday afternoon.

We bought sexy lingerie, body oils, and candles—that was all we needed to have a great time.

For your convenience, we provide a checklist at the end of this chapter. It includes all the accessories you might want for your weekend.

HIGHLY RECOMMENDED PERSONAL ITEMS

These are the few items that we believe will really enhance your weekend experience; you can virtually buy everything we mention here online.
Visit **www.thegreatsexweekend.com** to read about newest products, and getaway specials, as well as featured destinations that we discover that will enhance your weekend together.

NEW UNDERWEAR. His and hers lingerie are relatively inexpensive teasers. The sexier, the better. Finding sexy underwear for her is easy. If he always wears white Jockey briefs, buy colorful ones. If he always wears long boxers, consider buying the shorter, tighter variety.

LOTIONS AND MASSAGE OILS. Massage is an important addition to your weekend intimacy. These products are easy to find at most shopping malls. Bath stores like The Body Shop and Bath and Body Works carry a variety of scented lotions and oils. Lavender is particularly calming and citrus is uplifting. You'll also find these products on some of the websites we describe in Appendix 4.

We like the Kama Sutra products—especially the great honey dust powder!

CANDLES. Easy to find are scented candles to add gentle aromas as well as romantic light to your weekend interlude. As we said, candles not only help set a mood but they provide the most flattering lighting effect. Since most hotels no longer have ashtrays in your room, don't forget to pack a few candle holders for convenience and safety sake.

SCENTS. Although subtle, many people find smell is an important part of their sexual arousal. You might also want to have on hand some bath oils, bath salts, or bubble bath, nice bars of mildly scented soaps. Scents some road-testers said they liked included incense, lavender, vanilla, raspberry, or gardenia.

Although the aphrodisiac powers of essential oils are not proven, many people believe that certain scents do arouse, among them are jasmine, sandalwood, rose, and ylang-ylang. You can put a few drops in bathwater or mix them with safflower or almond oil to make your own aromatic massage oil.

I love blending scents. Experiment to see what you like. I like burning vanilla and strawberry scented candles together; sometimes I go for cinnamon with vanilla.

LUBRICANTS. These are useful when you are just touching each other during foreplay and essential for most women when engaging in frequent or prolonged intercourse. Especially if you use condoms, lubricants are needed to keep sex fun rather than irritating or painful. *Never use oil-based lubricants with*

24

condoms because oil causes rubber to disintegrate in a short time. Some favorite lubricants are Pink, Wet, Eros, KY's Intense, Astroglide, Sylk, and the manly-appealing Gun Oil. Most come in water-based and silicon-based; the latter is the longest lasting and the slickest that you can use.

CONDOMS. If you rely on condoms, be sure to stock up for the weekend. Buy lots of your favorite condoms, or use this as an opportunity to be more playful and buy an assortment, perhaps including lightly ribbed condoms or other designs that are out of the ordinary. Trojan has an innovative line-up including Ecstasy, Her Pleasure, and Bareskin, one of the newest and thinnest condoms on the market. Go to TrojanCondoms.com to check out the variety. Also, if you are considering anal sex, condoms are the best way to protect the health of *both* partners.

RELAXATION AIDS. Because we believe in the gift of massage, but also realize how tiring it can be to give one, we recommend you consider buying a Hitachi Magic Wand, an electric massager found online and in stores that sell vibrators and other sexual aids. Hitachi developed this as a bonafide massage tool, but women long ago happily discovered that its powerful smooth-shaped head does double duty as a vibrator. For the latter use, we recommend the "slow" speed and starting with a hand towel or pajamas between you and the vibrator until you get used to it.

SEX TOYS. The getaway weekend offers a perfect time to introduce sex toys into your bedroom, or try a new toy, if you already have one or more in your collection. If there's a sex boutique in your city and you don't mind being seen in it, getting ready for your weekend can be almost as much fun as the weekend itself.

Sneak away during an afternoon lunch hour or take a more leisurely after-dinner stroll through one of these stores. Just looking at the inventory in stores like Pleasure Chest in Los Angeles or Chicago, New York's Eve's Garden, San Francisco's Good Vibrations, Fascinations Super Store in Denver and Seattle's Babeland (also in NYC) can be an educational experience. Smaller cities have adult novelty boutiques, too; consult "adult shopping" in Yelp.com for your area.

If there are no stores of this type in your area, or if you don't want to be seen in a sex boutique, see our Appendix 4 for our favorite online websites where you can shop from your home discreetly. All transactions are strictly confidential, and these mail-order houses *never* sell, give, or trade any customer's name. Again, for your convenience, virtually everything from the condoms and lubes to the lingerie, vibrators, massage oils, sex checks, etc. can be found at websites like *goodvibes.com*.

An interesting note about who uses sex toys: According to a 1990s University of Chicago scientific survey, 16 percent of women and 23 percent of men between ages 18 and 44 find the idea of using sex toys appealing. But a very recent set of scientific studies done at Indiana University found that vibrator use is not only extremely common—roughly half of American women, and nearly as many men—but that its use is associated with good sexual health, increased desire and ease of orgasm (no, they're not addictive).

A popular adult sex toy website surveyed their own customers and found that they came from every race, religion (except Muslim), income bracket, and age group.

That company, The Xandria Collection, reported that vibrators (both battery and electric) and dildos were by far the most popular toys. Commonly beloved vibrators include "the rabbit" (a G-spot stimulator) and vibrating penis rings. The distant third favorite types of toys: restraint devices like handcuffs and blindfolds.

My husband came up with a clever idea. We didn't want to spend the money on restraints we weren't even sure that we'd like. So he suggested we try his workout "Power Bands" (they're like giant rubber bands connecting Velcro cuffs that were designed to add weight resistance during exercises). Wow. We both found being voluntarily "tied up' was very sexy.

SEX CHECKS. Courtesy of the generous people at Good Vibrations, we have included models of their Sex Checks from its Checkbook redeemable for sensual treats. Sex Checks are a way to give your partner the promise of something special, from "Sex in a Semi-Public Place" or an "Erotic Picnic in Bed" to "A Night of X-Rated Video Viewing—with total control of the remote" to "Unlimited Vibrator Induced Orgasms."

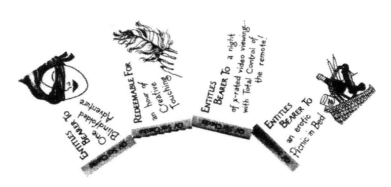

These days you can buy books of already printed Sex Checks at websites like goodvibrations.com Issued by the "World Bank of Savings and Love" their checkbook includes "30 IOU's and 30 UOME's, making it easy for you to get back what you give."

> *We liked the Sex Checks. They did encourage us to do things out of the ordinary. We combined the "Blindfolded Adventure" with the "Oral Pleasure Fest`` and really had fun.*

> *I probably would not have introduced my husband to my vibrator without the Sex Check, and he liked it! So I shared my other sex toys with him for the first time—I never had the nerve in the six years we've been together!*

NON-TOXIC BODY PAINTS. Any well-stocked toy shop or toy department should have a variety of nontoxic paints, including finger-paints as well as brush-on varieties. If you want to splurge, while indulging your sweet tooth, go to online and order the Kama Sutra Lovers' Paintbox, with 3 flavors of edible body chocolate plus brush.

Sight and Sound

PORTABLE SOUND SYSTEM. As stated earlier, music is an important part of setting the right mood. Download some especially romantic songs—or some rock'n'roll that will keep you movin'—on to your ipod. Don't forget to pack your docking station so you can have just the right soundtrack for your special weekend. Well-chosen music not only enhances a romantic atmosphere but the lyrics can provide another way to express sentiments to your partner that you might feel awkward actually saying.

> *Al Green from the 1970s was the sexiest soul singer ever He croons with such emotional fervor that his lyrics give me permission to be more open and romantic with my lover.*

VISUAL EROTICA. In chapter 5, we offer a range of choices, from light romantic comedies to sensual R-rated movies. Light pornography, if it intrigues you both, can be both entertaining and arousing. The better X-rated fare can improve your fantasy life as well as introduce ideas for new sexual techniques or settings.

If you want to purchase erotic dvd's that are appealing to female sensibilities, go to *www.goodvibes.com* where they recommend films that are women, or couple, friendly. If you don't have your own collection of erotica on your laptop, and you don't want to buy a new dvd, you might want to select a hotel that you know has a wide selection of videos-on-demand as an entertainment option.

Of course, we're Old School, so we still like books, too. One way to get in the mood, and to get inspired to do things that are out of the ordinary for you, is to look at some timeless books that show sex acts and all the position possibilities. We particularly like the Ann Hooper series on *The Ultimate Sexual Touch*, or her updated take on the *Kama Sutra*—or seek out a reprinting of the classic Indian version. To learn about how principles based in traditional Chinese medicine can improve your sex life, get Felice Duna's *Passion Play: Ancient Secrets for a Lifetime of Health and Happiness Through Sensational Sex*. We also still like all the editions of Alex Comfort's *The Joy of Sex*.

Feeding the Body—and Soul

FOODS OF LOVE. Have you ever told your partner that he or she looked good enough to eat? This is the time to make it happen. There are lots of foods that road-testers say they like to lick and nibble off their partners' body: your favorite chocolate sauce, pudding, whipped cream (some add figs, papaya, or mango, too). If there's some treat that you haven't used in years—or never dared to try—this is a good time to stock up.

SWEET LIBATIONS. If you've been saving a special bottle of wine or champagne for a special occasion, this might be it. It's a lot less expensive to bring your own liquor into a hotel; for wines or champagne, you need only an ice bucket. A few road-test couples mentioned they packed wine coolers for sunset or afternoon picnics. Of course, we caution people not to overdo it: A little liquor helps because it reduces inhibitions, but too much, and there goes the weekend.

OPTIONAL PERSONAL TOUCHES

EXCHANGING SMALL GIFTS. This is a nice way to start a special weekend with kindness. Gifts are not at all necessary, and many road-testers didn't give them and didn't miss them. We plant the idea just because a little gift can be a great antidote to the brisk and often insensitive pace of everyday life. If you like the idea but it adds to the burden of preparation, wait to buy each other souvenirs during your getaway weekend.

Gift Suggestions

- ♥ Sentimental cards with a few romantic lines that really capture the way you feel about your partner
- ♥ Flowers for her (or him, if he likes them)
- ♥ A perfume for her or cologne for him that you both find arousing
- ♥ Mix of music that you know will be appreciated
- ♥ Lingerie
- ♥ Book of erotic stories. Here are a few recommendations: *On the Wings of Eros: Nightly Readings for Passion and Romance*; *The Mammoth Book of Erotica*; Susie Bright's *Best American Erotica: 15th Anniversary Edition*; Marcy Sheiner's *Herotica 7: New American Fiction by Women*; *Erotique Noire/Black Erotica*; Lonnie Barbach's *The Erotic Edge: 22 Erotic Stories for Couples,* and *Slow Hand: Women Writing Erotica.*

You can give some of the illustrated books we mentioned, like *The Kama Sutra* or any of the *Joy of Sex* editions as a titillating gift.

> *Since it was my husband's birthday, I gave him a pair of tight, soft, comfortable fleece pants. He looked so good in them that they definitely helped set the mood.*

> *I sent him flowers. The card in the flowers contained a suggestive poem and I signed off, "Can't wait to pleasure you."*

> *He got silk boxers; I got some CDs from my favorite artists.*

> *I bought him flowers and he got me peach bubble bath. These thoughtful gifts got our sex vacation off to a good start.*

> *I bought him a card. My husband liked it but said, "Let's get to the sex!"*

> *I had flowers sent to the room so they'd be waiting for her. Then I told her there was one more surprise somewhere in the room. I had slipped a heart-shaped pendant under one of the pillows. When she finally found it, I dropped down on one knee and asked her to marry me all over again. Any other time, I would've felt silly. This weekend I gave myself permission to be all-out romantic, and she loved it.*

The Great Sex Weekend
Checklist and Shopping List

_____ Colored light bulbs (blue or pint bulbs like the ones they use on *Playboy* photo shoots to set a mood)

_____ Scented candles & candleholders

_____ Flowers

_____ Cards/notes

_____ New lingerie

_____ Body lotions/massage oil

_____ Bath salts; bubble bath; bath oils

_____ Lubricants

_____ Fun condoms

_____ Hitachi Magic Wand (electric massager/vibrator)

_____ Sex toys (Sex Checks, restraints, etc.)

_____ Edible body paints

_____ Docking station for your iPod

_____ Laptop (for erotic entertainment, NOT for email!)

_____ DVDs of favorite romantic movies or erotica

_____ Books of erotic readings or sexual acts

_____ Chocolate sauce, whipped cream, or other "body" food

_____ Champagne, wine, or other alcohol

_____ Personal gifts

CHAPTER 3

Friday Night

*The anticipation of starting our weekend
created an aura that was visible to my friends,
several of whom remarked that I was glowing.*

It's Friday and your weekend is about
to begin. Give yourself time to make a mental
transition from all your obligations, finish your
packing, and make final preparations. Your goal is to
have everything taken care of by dinnertime.

When you check into your hotel, set up your
candles, portable sound system, flowers, and anything
else you brought to set the atmosphere and personalize
the room.

You may feel ready to make love as soon as you
enter the bedroom. We suggest holding back. Dress for
dinner, changing clothes privately. Act as though you
were getting ready for a date. A woman can dab
perfume or cologne in sensual places like the back of
her neck or between her breasts. It's always nice to
surprise the senses in unexpected ways. If you dare,
wear sexier underwear than you normally choose.

*I wore fishnet stockings under my dress and no
underwear. It was freezing that night in Denver, so I
suffered a hit for my surprise—but it was worth it!*

Now you're ready to start the program. Keep our guiding principle in mind: Everything is optional. There isn't time to do it all. We have rated some activities "highly recommended," but do the exercises that appeal to both of you. We arranged the exercises to achieve maximum effect, but this is not a military manual. You may wish to reverse order, skip around, move activities from one day to the next, and so forth. What's important is to relax, have fun, feel close, and lavish the kind of attention on each other that you did in the early days of your relationship.

EXERCISE 1: An Early-Evening Walk

*Fresh air always raises our spirits. Walking,
even in the rain, felt invigorating, intimate, and
refreshing.*

Take a leisurely walk for about a half hour. Try
not to talk shop, or about the kids. Instead, hold hands.
Research shows that holding hands helps create a sense
of happiness and connectedness. Here are some ideas:

♥ Reminisce about your first days spent together.
♥ Recall the first time you had sex. What do you
remember most affectionately about your

experience or the first morning that you woke up together?

♥ Remember your first weekend getaway.

We brought the DVD from our commitment ceremony to the hotel. We hadn't seen it for years, so it was great to reminisce.

♥ Tell each other what you like most about each other. Surprise your partner by sharing traits that you find endearing. Tell your partner about qualities you take the most pleasure or pride in about yourself.

We talked about how our sex life had been on hold for a while and how we really need to work on it. We also talked about music and what we liked. He told me how beautiful I was.

Friday Night Dinner

Think of this meal as foreplay. Consider room service for an added touch of luxury and privacy. You might want to use your candles for an added romantic touch. If you choose to dine out, find a restaurant that will provide the most romantic atmosphere. The back of the local *Zagat Guide* lists the most romantic restaurants in the area.

Dinner Talk

It was fun to have suggested topics to talk about. We made it a game to propose topics we'd never thought about before.

Here are some additional topics for dinner conversation:

- ♥ A dream vacation: Even if it's years away, plan its basic shape. Where would you both like to go?
- ♥ Reminisce in detail about the best vacation you ever took together. What made it so special?
- ♥ Take turns describing the things you like about the way your partner makes love to you.

We really enjoyed all the talking exercises. We got to thinking, remembering, and sharing with each other; these were the most intimate moments we had had in a long time.

Stay in your personal comfort zone for public displays of affection, but be flirtatious with each other. Touch hands, or discreetly graze a breast or a thigh. A little shoeless footwork under the table is always nice, too. A few short kisses set a nice mood. A little exhibitionism can be a turn-on if you both like it.

EXERCISE 2: Undressing Each Other

That first night, maybe the sexiest thing she did was to undress tantalizingly and slowly.

A scientific survey revealed that both men and women found watching a partner undress to be as appealing sexually as receiving oral sex. That doesn't mean everyone likes to be watched while undressing. Still, if you can stand the scrutiny, it is usually very sexy to slowly and flirtatiously strip for your partner. Or if it would make you less self-conscious, undress each other. It doesn't matter who starts. Take your time and take turns taking off one piece of clothing at a time.

EXERCISE *3*: Kissing

We don't spend enough time kissing. When we really concentrated on it, things started to heat up.

Kissing is very important. Among women's top sexual complaints is that they don't get kissed enough. But this is an easy problem to fix. Pretend that this is your first experience kissing. Be tentative and exploratory. Try kissing in ways that are not usually the way you two kiss. Kiss a little longer, a little lighter, or a little harder.

We pretended that we were strangers kissing for the first time. Delicious.

We giggled and couldn't do this exercise the first time we tried it. But we tried again when we were really turned on, and then it was fabulous.

Of course, this isn't really the first time you've kissed, so one or both of you might feel a little silly—even laugh. That's understandable. But take a few seconds to say which type of kisses you really liked the most.

EXERCISE 4: Pleasuring

The touching exercises helped me find places on my husband that I would never have thought to be erogenous zones—like the backs of his knees.

Pleasuring is a highly recommended technique some therapists use to slow down the rush to intercourse and concentrate on sensuality. It also helps people rediscover the full range of erotic stimulation beyond the obvious erogenous zones. Pleasuring involves exploring to test every possible part of the body for sensitivity before any conventionally erotic zones can be touched. Erotic pleasuring is allowed everywhere except *inside* the body.

You and your partner should take turns throughout this exercise, giving a few minutes to each body area described below. Linger longer if you're both really enjoying it. Move your fingers much more slowly than usual to increase the intensity for both of you. Ask your partner what feels good and what does not.

41

Start at the toes. Touch your partner's toes lightly using one or a few fingers, then caress the toes and feet with your whole hand. Move up the leg, touching ankles, calves, and inner and outer thighs—first with the light touch, then harder. Keep asking for feedback; the person being touched answers with 'That's great," or 'That tickles,' or "Harder, please." If you are responding, be sure to say "That's perfect" or "Just right" when it is.

Now start on the back. Concentrate on the buttocks, then move up to the lower then upper back and neck. Massage the hairline, head, and ear-lobes. Ask for a response.

Now move to the front, but skip the genitals for now. Lightly touch the stomach, chest, and nipples; you can use more pressure on the front shoulder area. Continue to talk about how every part of the exercise feels.

> *What turned him on the most was when I lightly touched his entire body with the front of my fingernails.*

If you're really enjoying this exercise, you can start all over with substituting light kisses, licking, or sucking on some of the body parts declared "sensitive." This time move from top to bottom. Or you may want to exchange full body massages, as we describe in Chapter 5. Or move right into the next exercise.

EXERCISE 5: Eye Contact (Highly Recommended)

> *The most erotic experience was practicing eye contact Friday night. We usually close our eyes and give in to the feelings during foreplay But looking at each other again really heightened the intimacy.*

It has been said that the eyes are the windows to the soul. According to sex therapist David Schnarsch, eyes are also the gateway to intimacy, and most couples deny themselves greater intimacy because they do not look at each other during lovemaking. Take a few minutes and, while touching each other, look into each other's eyes and draw out the trust, emotion, and vulnerability that exist between you. If you feel like you have to look away, do so, but try to return each other's gaze as much as possible.

MOVING TOWARD ORGASM

> *We held off from orgasm. Bringing each other almost to climax hut making each other wait only intensified the experience when we finally let each other go.*

We fully expect that after a week of abstinence, most of you will want an orgasm by Friday night, fine. But we recommend using this time to enjoy a lot more foreplay than usual. It slows things down, allowing you to rediscover each other's body. It's a break from "same old, same old" and will also heighten passion.

Having to abstain from intercourse really brought us together. We did other things to please each other. When we finally had it, we really appreciated it and our response was much more intense.

Of course, you can choose to have intercourse whenever you like on Friday night, but for those of you willing to delay, here are a few optional exercises. We encourage you to take this time to arouse each other by different forms of foreplay and satisfy each other in ways you may skip in your usual sex life together.

OPTIONAL EXERCISE 6: Touching the Genitals

One way you can explore the way your partner likes to be touched is to watch your partner touch him- or herself. This isn't for everyone, but you can learn a lot about your partner's preference for pressure, rhythm, and technique if he or she is willing to show you.
Of course, the focus isn't on having an orgasm. Just enjoy the exercises. Being less goal-oriented switches the focus to sensuality, which is quite pleasurable, even without an orgasm.

OPTION: Touching Her to Orgasm

Maintaining eye contact while touching her may intensify her excitement and arouse you as well. Trace your fingers on the insides of her thighs (checking to see if this feels good or if it tickles). Let her feel how you are totally absorbed and taken with her. Start stroking her labia very, very gently. Ask her if she would like anything harder or softer.

Remember, this is not lovemaking as usual. You are rediscovering her body. Tonight marks a change of pace from the usual routine. So ask her every so often about rhythm and where and how hard she wants to be touched.

Gently put two fingers inside the lips on each side of the clitoral shaft, and trace the opening around the clitoris; you can *gently* squeeze the clitoris between your fingers. Don't put a finger inside or on the clitoris for any length of time until everything is quite wet. You can wet your finger by putting it in your mouth or you can use a small amount of lubricant, if needed. Then slowly penetrate with a finger while using the other hand to very gently touch around the clitoral area, asking her if she wants you to touch the clitoris directly or just around it. Ask her what she likes. Tell her about your own excitement to help build her enjoyment and passion.

> *My partner touched me very slowly, gently, and really explored my whole genital area. I felt like he didn't miss touching anything. It was very sensual and ultimately made me extremely turned on.*

Be slow, patient, and luxurious with your fingers. Be consistent when erotic tension is mounting. Sometimes when women get close to orgasm, they lose the climax if anything—the rhythm, the area being touched, the strength of pressure—changes. But some women need stronger stimulation at exactly this time because when a woman approaches an orgasm, her clitoris slightly retracts.

When she seems close to orgasm, ask her to tell you (whisper, full voice, scream—whatever) if she wants you to keep doing what you're doing. That way there's no mistaking what she wants, and she'll have enough confidence to go over the edge to an ecstatic orgasm.

OPTION: Giving Her Oral Sex to Orgasm

If you are adding oral sex, go down on your partner after you have stimulated her with your hand. If she feels self-conscious, tell her how much you love touching her and how much you want to be between her legs.

Many women can achieve orgasm through oral stimulation only when they feel safe, comfortable, and desirable. Some women may feel inhibited because they fear that their genitals are somehow unpleasant to taste or smell. If it takes a woman a long time to climax, she may get concerned that her partner is getting tired or bored, or worse yet, will stop just before her orgasm. Let her know that she tastes good, and that she can take as long as she likes. The vast majority of men—nine out of ten, according to one major survey—say they enjoy giving oral sex to women. It's a great turn-on if she really believes you are very aroused and into giving her pleasure.

Partners should know that the whole genital area can be very sensitive and almost anything will feel good once a woman is fully aroused. Take lots of time to explore her with your mouth. Gently lick and suck on the entire area—the vaginal lips, the clitoris, as well as the area above and below it (the small area between the vaginal area and the anus can be very erotic). Alternate sucking and licking. If you know she likes penetration during oral sex, when she's wet, penetrate her vagina with one or more fingers. If she's really excited and relaxed, this is going to feel fabulous.

Instead of penetration, she may prefer you keep touching her with both hands. Use them to reach up and gently massage her breasts or tug lightly on her nipples. Unless you know your partner likes her breasts to be grasped roughly—or she tells you to do that—use a light touch.

OPTION: Anal Stimulation

If you know she enjoys anal stimulation or she's indicated that she would like to try it for the first time on this weekend, you can rub the anus externally, or, with a lot of lubricant, gently penetrate it with the tip of one finger. Slowly move the tip of the finger in and out. Ask her if that feels good. If she likes it, move the finger in a little farther (make sure your nails are filed and short). If she's not sure, or says no, don't try it again during this session unless she asks for it. Be cautious. If you have touched the anal area, thoroughly wash your hands before touching her vagina again. You don't want to transfer bacteria from one area to another.

OPTION: Touching Him to Orgasm

With the man on his back, start gently stroking his penis. A light lubricating lotion can be used if he likes the feel of it. The entire penis has nerve endings, but the areas most sensitive to touch are the glans (the head of the penis), the corona (the ridge of the glans), and the frenum (the strip of skin connecting the glans to the shaft on the underside of the penis). Gently trace the fingers across these areas, then down the shaft of the penis. Gently put the penis shaft between your thumb and your forefinger (or use the thumb and two or three fingers) and apply gentle but firm pressure while stroking it. Ask your partner how much pressure he likes, and if he wants one hand on the shaft or would prefer you put it between both. Ask him how he feels until he tells you what you are doing is just right.

Ask your partner if he wants his testicles touched, and if so, how. Many men like to have their testicles lightly stroked or cupped.

OPTION: Giving Him Oral Sex to Orgasm

A lot of men say their most intense orgasms take place during oral sex. This may be the case for your partner, and you may want him to climax this way tonight. If you like giving him that pleasure, tell him what you are about to do and how much it excites you to do it. This will turn him on more.

If neither partner has much experience with oral sex, this would be a good time to experiment. But don't force it. This is true for both partners. If unequal desire for oral sex has been an issue between you, don't make it an issue tonight. Perhaps come back to this option tomorrow when more experimental urges might prevail. Or let your partner know that you might be ready to try this next time you use this book for a weekend getaway.

If you decide to have oral sex, take it slowly and easily to begin with, and take a break if you feel tired or uncomfortable. You can relax your jaw by alternating sucking with licking the highly sensitive parts of the penis. You might vary the degree of suction you use, and ask what your partner likes best.

This should be a turn-on for both partners. Giving oral sex for too long can become more of a chore than a pleasure to many women, so do it as long as it gives you both enjoyment. Watching him ejaculate can be really sexy for both partners.

> *I found it exciting to pleasure myself with my hand while my partner licked and sucked around my genitals. When it was my turn to go down on her, it was exciting for me to lick her while she touched her clitoris.*

OPTION: Anal Touching for Him

Ask him if he would like you to touch his anus. Or you might just put your finger there to stimulate the exterior of the opening, then ask if he likes the feel of it. Some men like penetration by one or more fingers. Ask him if he would like to try. If so, make sure you have plenty of lubrication on your finger. Make sure your nails are filed and short.

Ease your finger in a little bit at a time, maybe just a fingertip for the first time. If the man is tensing up, don't push. If he is relaxed, you'll feel it and be able to slide in easily. It is best not to try this before the man is intensely turned on. Even so, anal stimulation may do nothing at all for him. If he says he doesn't like it, stop.

On the other hand, some men and women who are doing this for the first time will be surprised how much a man can enjoy this because if he relaxes enough for your finger to be in (and a little downward) and far enough to feel the smooth surface of his prostate gland, stroking that gland is always enough to produce an unbelievably intense orgasm.

OPTION: SAVING YOUR ORGASMS FOR INTERCOURSE

> *It was exciting to know that our kissing and foreplay would not immediately lead to intercourse. More time was spent exploring, and it forced us to continue our other activities. Then, when intercourse did come, it was overwhelming. You don't take anything for granted if it isn't always available.*

After a week of abstinence, some couples will prefer to do abbreviated versions of the above exercises just as fore-play, and save their orgasm for intercourse. Of course, some people are not going to want their orgasm any other way.

> *I started touching him while saying let's not do it until tomorrow. I said it to get him crazy, but I was just teasing. No way I was waiting any longer. I wanted him inside of me tonight.*

AFTER ORGASM

After orgasm, take a few moments to express affection. Some people like to talk, while others just want to be quiet. For this special weekend, see if your partner will talk about what he or she really liked. If you're not sleepy, you may want to order up room service for a midnight snack, or go get a glass of dessert wine in the hotel's bar. Don't set the alarm. And if one of you wakes up during the night and reaches over, don't discourage it. More intimacy is fine if you're both interested.

CHAPTER 4

Saturday Morning and Afternoon

We like sex in the morning. We wake up together and we feel more rested, more sensuous, and then we can make it as long or as short as we like.

WAKING UP TOGETHER

Enjoy sleeping in Saturday morning. You are having an affair with each other this weekend. The mood is romantic and out of the ordinary. Kiss, snuggle; don't just jump out of bed. Think of the following recommendations as optional recipe ingredients for a great morning. We offer one plan for the morning that we know worked well for the road-test couples who tried it.

INGREDIENT #1: BREAKFAST IN BED

We recommend breakfast in bed as one way to maintain the weekend's warm and sensual feeling. If you are in a hotel, order up something special like a mimosa (orange juice and champagne) with your food.

INGREDIENT #2: BATHING TOGETHER

*After we were both soapy, we put our arms
around each other and moved our bodies up
and down against each other very gently. The
feel of gliding bodies is very sensual.*

Take a sensual shower together. If you like, use
an invigorating loofah sponge or soft-mesh cleansing
puff on each other. Have on hand a few special scented
bar soaps that smell of vanilla, strawberry, papaya,
gardenia—whatever pleases you. Let all your senses
participate in this shower. Make it feel exotic and sexy.

Take turns soaping each other up. Take your
time and pay attention to each part of your partner's
body. Massage the shampoo into his or her hair, using
your fingers to knead neck and shoulders, too. Does he
or she want more or less pressure? *Practice asking for
and giving feedback all weekend long.*

Once your partner is in a state of pleasure
meltdown, move your hands over the rest of the body,
starting from the top down. Let your hands linger on
each other's chest, breasts, lower back, and legs.
When you touch the genital areas, touch to arousal but
don't get carried away. Be careful about where you put
soapy fingers. If you put them inside the vagina or anus,
the soap might sting.

After you're all soaped up, take turns slowly
rinsing each other's hair. It's really sensual to kiss each
other with the water dripping down your face. Pat each
other dry and go back to bed in your towels if you're up
for the next ingredient. This would be a perfect time to
wear any new lingerie that you bought just for this
weekend. Try to notice your partner's change of
appearance and be admiring. Saying how your partner

looks to you always makes an experience more wonderful.

INGREDIENT #3: ROLE REVERSAL MORNING

> *Loved it! It gave me permission to be aggressive, and he could relax since he did not have the responsibility to initiate.*

> *Speaking from the male perspective, I am definitely more turned on when my partner initiates intimacy.*

From after breakfast to just before dinner, all physical and sexual overtures are to be initiated by the female. *(Note to all couples:* Whichever partner initiates sex less frequently should be the one who takes the initiative for this part of today. In most heterosexual relationships, that's the woman, but if this is not the case in your situation, then have the man initiate.)

> *I initiate 99 percent of the time when we have sex. I am usually the one who takes control of our sex. So my husband needed to be the initiator today.*

While most men are used to being the sexual initiator and enjoy it, always being the one responsible for sex can also be a burden and poses the risk of rejection. Many men don't get to explore the side of their personality that might like being guided through a sexual encounter that was shaped by someone else's imagination or pacing. Also, men often express the wish to be desired. When his partner "takes over," a man knows how much she wants him— but apparently this doesn't happen often enough. Surveys have shown that infrequent initiation of sex by women is among men's top complaints about what's wrong with their sex life.

Women have traditionally been advised not to be too aggressive with male partners. Many women and men see aggressive moves as unfeminine or threatening to the male's sense of control. Women get to enjoy feeling "irresistible," so why shouldn't men? We are going to encourage women to experiment with a little sexual dominance just to see how erotic it can be.

He lies down on the bed and his partner gives him a short back massage. Next, lie facing each other, hold each other, and talk about how you would like to make love. She should decide on a position for intercourse, like the ones discussed later in this chapter. Since the woman is leading, let her decide how and what to touch first.

Exotic Option for Birth Control

Sometimes couples use one of the textured condoms just for the fun of how it feels. Putting on a condom is a bit of an art, too. The male should lie on his back and tell his partner how to place the condom on the head of the penis and slowly roll it down until it covers the full shaft. This can be done very slowly and seductively, while touching the scrotum and nibbling on his nipples.

I placed the condom on the tip of his penis in the usual way and then unrolled it by drawing the penis into my mouth and pushing the rolled edge all the way down with my lips. This works best with the flavored lubricated variety.

If the female partner is not very wet naturally, supplement with a great lubricant. In chapter 2 we recommended several different water-based ones if you are using a latex condom or silicone, if you are not some people like products made with aloe vera (like Gun Oil)—which also makes the genitals feel smooth and silky.

Applying lubrication can be a sexy part of foreplay, so you may want to use it even if the woman is naturally very moist. Each should put a little bit on the other partner, gently touching different parts of the genitalia until each person is slick and aroused. A slow, sensual approach changes an ordinary act into an erotic one.

I really enjoyed your instructions for how my husband should use a lubricant on me. I used to feel like a piece of bread being slathered with butter. This approach was a real turn-on.

Beyond the Missionary Position

We would like you to consider trying at least one, and perhaps all four, of our suggested alternative positions for lovemaking sometime this weekend. Even if you end up in your usual position— whatever that is—this would be a good time to also try something new or a position you use less often than others.

Woman on Top

We recommend a woman-on-top position as a starting point. In this position the woman has greater control over the depth of penetration and pace of thrusting. There are several variations on this theme. Some require more physical strength or agility.

NUMBER ONE- He's lying down and she's on top, facing him. She can be on her knees with forearms extended. This allows less depth of penetration, but it is easier to sustain for a longer time.

NUMBER TWO— Partners are on a chair and she is sitting on his lap, facing him. Penetration is deep, but thrusting is limited because you are so close. Done slowly, this can be a very sensual position.

NUMBER THREE- He's lying on his back. She can squat over him, balance on her feet and have a lot of leverage lowering herself down on him. (She needs good balance and strength to do this for any length of time. It can also be tricky if the bed is not very firm, so this might be better done on the floor.)

ADVANTAGES OF WOMAN-ON-TOP POSITIONS

These positions are face-to-face. You can look deeply into each other's eyes and see each other's expressions. Both partners can lean over and kiss each other. The man can touch the woman's clitoris, her breasts and nipples, or grip her buttocks. The woman can touch and gently pinch the man's nipples. Or she can lay back, touching the scrotum from time to time. She can also easily reach for more lubricant if she needs it. One added bonus: these positions aid in delaying the man s orgasm.

We suggest a lot of clitoral touching, either by the male, the woman touching herself, or both. Let the woman control penetration and pace; she should keep shifting angles to see which one feels the best to her and her partner. Try moving the shaft of the penis against the pubic bone, then as far away from it as possible. Touch the clitoris in long strokes or in short ones. Touch the labia gently as they touch the penis shaft. In the Number One position women can stroke the penis as it goes in and out, occasionally reaching back to stroke the testicles and inner thighs. See how many different sensations can be experienced, and make sure the other person knows what really feels good to you, what you would like repeated or sustained—or remembered when you return to lovemaking in everyday life.

Spoon Position

This position is a very cuddly way of making love. There is a lot of close contact for the bodies, and it is easy for a long time. The woman's back is pressed against the man's front and he is entering from the rear.

Although the couple cannot see each other unless the man lifts his head and leans over the woman, nor can the woman easily touch the man, there is a lot of full contact with this position. The woman can relax and just be made love to. The man's hands are free to caress the woman's breasts and genitals, and the woman's hands are free for her to touch her clitoris or labia. The woman can control depth of penetration. This is a good position for women who prefer shallow penetration. And finally, this position is not too physically taxing and the man, especially, doesn't have to worry about getting tired out.

Rear Entry

> *We tried them all, but our favorite is the rear entry with my wife's back really arched. It allows the penis to penetrate deeper.*

This is a position that men seem to like a lot. There are three main variations:

NUMBER ONE- The woman is on her stomach, arms outstretched, palms down, or she is propped up on her elbows A pillow can be placed under her pelvis to raise her slightly. This position is easy for her if she can find a comfortable position. The man is holding his weight by outstretching his arms, his hands on each side of her hips, his legs between her legs and outstretched behind him.

NUMBER TWO—The woman is on her knees, either with straight arms or on her elbows. The straight arms require more strength. The man is on his knees  if he's on the bed, too, or he's on his feet if standing at bed's edge, and his hands are either on his partner's back or, for maximum penetration, on her buttocks. In this latter position, he is straight-backed, moving his hips straight into her.

NUMBER THREE—The man is seated on a chair and the woman sits on him, facing away from him. She has a lot of control over penetration; he doesn't have to work very hard.

Men especially find this position erotic, because it allows them to set the pace of their thrusts. Some women occasionally like giving this sense of control to their partner. Some men love what, for them, is optimally deep penetration.

Many men find looking at their partner's buttocks and watching the penis move in and out to be extremely erotic. Being able to see one s self in a mirror is a bonus. The man can reach around and easily stroke the clitoris and vulva. This is very exciting when combined with holding the buttocks and thrusting. While this position is highly stimulating to many men, it also gives them some control against rapid ejaculation because they can easily withdraw by lifting her a little when they get close to orgasm.

Face-to-Face, Side by Side

We like face-to-face, side by side. It is the most intimate to us because we have our hands and arms free to hold each other.

In this position the man and woman face each other, looking into each other's eyes, and have  almost full body contact. The woman puts her leg over the man's hip, allowing him to enter her at an angle. Her arm is around his shoulder, while one of the man's arms is stretched out under his head or is helping to support his body. The other arm is free, and the hand can touch her breasts or reach down and touch her genital area.

While the woman has only a little maneuvering room and might find holding her position over him tiring, this one is not physically taxing. Because the couple is face-to-face, they can maintain more frequent eye contact, and kiss easily and often during lovemaking. This position allows medium penetration, more than in the spoon position but not as much as woman above or man behind. It allows a lot of contact with the labia and the clitoris, and because it is a more unusual position, it might be stimulating just because it allows penetration in a new angle.

The woman can stroke the man's face, touch his chest, and move away a little bit and touch his penis as it glides in and out. She has some control over depth of penetration, and there is mutual control over the pace of thrusting.

WHY TRY THESE POSITIONS?

It might seem unimportant to you to experiment with many or all of these positions but our recommendations are based on a scientific finding: Research shows that one of things that separates couples who keep the passion alive versus those who don't is that the former try new positions for intercourse as a fun and easy way to keep variety in their sex lives.

Obviously you can try a few new positions, then have your orgasm in the tried-and-true way, but today we're going to recommend that you climax in a new position (or at least a less familiar one)

Interlude: Time-Out After Sex

After you have had a really terrific orgasm, we want you to take it easy. A couple cannot live by sex alone. Part of any intimate vacation is varying the main event with other pleasures. We recommend an all-afternoon break. Almost anything you enjoy doing together is fine. However, we strongly suggest not choosing a competitive activity, such as tennis, even if you normally enjoy playing against each other. We don't want a bad game to spoil anyone's mood. (You don't want to engage in a very strenuous activity. Keep your outings brief and leisurely.)

- Shop together for fun (e.g., go antique or bargain hunting).
- Take in an upbeat funny or romantic matinee
- Go to an arboretum or public park
- Have lunch at a wonderful cafe or view restaurant.

- Go for an easy hike and a picnic
- Explore some place new area together. Visit a museum together or stroll through a few art galleries.
- Rest by the hotel's pool or Jacuzzi
- Take a drive in the country
- Go horseback riding.
- Go ice-skating or in-line skating.

We took our afternoon break touring the chocolate factory in Las Vegas—chocolate is one of our favorite aphrodisiacs. We came home and took a nap in each other's arms.

LATE AFTERNOON: TAKE IT EASY

We combined our afternoon break and rest time by napping cuddled in a blanket in the sun at the beach.

Depending on the time of day and your own preferences, you might save time at the end of the day for a nap. Naps are not only physically restorative, but quieting your minds together creates more intimacy. In any case, take some time to relax before getting ready for dinner.

CHAPTER 5

Saturday Evening

I surprised him by bringing new lingerie and a feather boa to wear with a push-up bra and high heels to do a striptease. He surprised me by bringing our camcorder and set it up to project my striptease onto the TV screen. I loved watching myself. It was a great turn-on for both of us.

You've had your day out, and maybe a nap, too. We hope you feel refreshed and ready for dinner. We suggest a little pre-dinner verbal foreplay.

HORS D'OEUVRES: VERBAL FOREPLAY BEFORE DINNER

EXERCISE I: Exchange Wish List and Sex Checks
(Highly Recommended)

Over a relaxing drink, talk about plans for this evening and Sunday. What would you like to do that you haven't done yet? What would your partner like to try? Is there anything that you would like to repeat? Each person makes a wish list. This is also a good time to exchange the Sex Checks discussed in chapter 2.

You could also make your *own* wish list by creating a personalized IOU and exchanging as many as you like now. You can have some fun by giving your partner a signed blank IOU as a playful open-ended invitation. Your partner gets a fantasy fulfilled, while you get the delight of a spontaneous surprise. You can then decide whether you want to grant the wish or redeem a check or IOU tonight or tomorrow, or sometime after the weekend, as a way to carry over new ideas into real life.

Personal Fantasy I.O.U.

EXERCISE 2: Swapping Fantasies

What are some of the things that you think about when you fantasize? (You don't really want to upset your partner by naming other people or admitting you sometimes pretend your partner is someone else while making love.) Tell your partner why the imagery you describe is so arousing for you.

Describe which images you want to keep only as fantasy and which ones you might want to act out a little—or a lot.

This exercise can be a bit risky, because there are some fantasies that shouldn't be revealed. However, the better you know and understand each other—and the more nonjudgmental you and your partner are—the more risks you can take. Sharing fantasies can be an intimate experience because sharing details requires and builds trust, while showing what turns you on.

> *He told me that he pictured me going down on him while we're driving on an empty desert highway. I said someday I'd love to have sex in a hotel jacuzzi late at night, knowing that other guests might be watching from their windows.*

> *I told him that I frequently fantasized that we're making love outdoors. When we got back from dinner, we had sex on a blanket on the bathroom floor with the heat lamp and pretended that we were outside in the hot sun.*

If you or your partner—individually or together—look at erotica online for arousal, this might be a perfect time to share and show each other what turns you on. While most research on cybersex focuses on the negative effects on the tiny minority of users who are addicted, newer research shows that most casual recreational users report mostly positive effects on their intimate relationships.

Both men and women say online 'porn' has made them more open to try new things and has made it easier for them to talk about what they want sexually with their partner. Some couples who use it together say it has resulted in more frequent and better quality sex.

DINNER: VERBAL FOREPLAY AND MORE.   .

Pick a special restaurant for tonight. Dress like you're going on a date, because you are! At this dinner, celebrate your closeness. Design your evening in one of two ways: You can make the evening non-sexual but romantic, or you can make it sexual and playful. No matter which option you choose, this evening is a good time to exchange great relationship stories and enjoy being together. You might want to recount a romantic memory, or recollect the best sex you've ever had together and why it was so good.

OPTION: A Dinner Game—*Fantasy Role-Playing*

Role-playing allows both of you to explore different parts of your imaginations that you wouldn't normally play out in real life. So try playacting as someone else. The biggest challenge is to keep yourself from feeling stupid or "breaking out of character." Still, if you can agree that you are in this "play" together, this exercise can be sexier than you might at first imagine. It's like having an affair without violating promises of monogamy.

In the most satisfying role-playing, your character's words and actions should come forth without inhibition. If you start the role-playing in a public place, you are more likely to carry through with the scenario. (Also, having an audience for your bold flirtation with a "total stranger" can be a terrific turn-on.) In private, try to include positions and sex acts that the characters you are playing would want but that you might be reluctant to try as "yourselves."

Keep in mind that whatever your partner does, this is a game. It's acting—like in the movies—and you're merely trying on another person's reality for a little while. If you have never done this before, pick a scenario that seems emotionally comfortable. And if you crack up laughing a few times, great; but then pull yourself together and continue. The idea is to be playful, titillating, and most of all, to have fun. Here are a few scenarios you might enjoy:

THE SEDUCTION. You are meeting each other for the first time. Walk separately into a restaurant for dinner and sit down at different tables. Pretend that you are strangers who start eyeing each other. One of you can walk over and introduce yourself. Or ask the food server to pass the other person a note saying how attractive you find him or her. The interaction with your server helps keep you in character. The person who receives the note can either motion the sender to come over or walk to the sender's table, say "hello," and sit down. Begin to flirt with each other. You can imagine that this is the beginning of a great love affair, or just a prelude to one stolen evening of pure lust.

> *I always thought my fiancé was a tad reticent, but he had a surprise in store for me. He walked away to the bar for our drinks and came back someone else! He began role-playing and all of the sudden there was this lovely man trying to pick me up. We were still ourselves, but we were strangers. He offered to buy me a drink and asked permission to join*

*me. We flirted and laughed and made small
talk for a couple of hours. We discovered the
freedom to talk about things the way you do to
someone you may never see again. He told me
things about "his relationship" that he had
never said before. What delicious revelations.
He actually expressed feelings I suspected
were inside of him but were kept hidden for
years.*

*We pretended we just met and had instant
chemistry. We went back to "his place."
Somewhere in the middle of the great sex, we
became ourselves again and continued the
lovemaking with lovely familiarity.*

SEX FOR SALE. Make believe one of you is "for
hire." He could be an elegant escort, or she a high-
priced, exclusive call girl. He could be a young man
having his first sexual experience with a mature
"woman of the world." Or it's her first time, so she
picked a Don Juan to introduce her to the mysteries of
sex.

*I couldn't believe how much he looked like an
"escort." He came to the door in an elegant
Italian suit. The hottest part was dancing; he
had a hard-on, his body never left mine, and
he kept asking me what I wanted and then
told me how he could give it to me.*

LIVES OF THE RICH AND FAMOUS. One of you
can pretend to be a famous actor, rock star, athlete, or
model whom you both find sexy; the other can be the
"admirer" who is selected for "quick" intimacy. You

come up to him or her in a restaurant for an autograph. The "star" shows immediate and unmistakable interest in you. Or both of you can be famous and you are trying to explore your attraction while avoiding the prying eyes and cameras of your fans and paparazzi. You want to be intimate, but of course everyone is watching. Eventually, you separately sneak back to your private hideaway.

AFTER DINNER CHOICES. We don't want you to feel as if you have embarked on an exhausting sexual marathon. Unless you have turned each other on so much that you want more, more, more, you might want to return to your hotel room and just cuddle and be close tonight. Some road-testers had the energy and desire to go out after dinner, and chose activities consistent with the weekend theme of trying things that are a bit out of the ordinary.

> *My husband surprised me by taking me to a strip club! I'd never been to one before. He brought twenty dollars in singles to tip the dancers, then invited a beautiful young woman to join us at our table, which was arousing for both of us. We stayed for about an hour and enjoyed watching the women be seductive, and I picked up some stripping tips to use later that night.*

If you don't want another sexual exercise, but you do want some more stimulation before going to sleep, we have a couple of suggestions:

OPTION: Enjoy a Movie Together in the Comfort of Bed

There might be a movie on demand that interests you; pick something light and romantic, or very sexy. Or you might have brought a favorite romantic movie that you haven't seen in a long time.

Here are some old classics that include sexy scenes you might like:

Body Heat	*Risky Business*
Basic Instinct	*Sex, Lies, and Videotape*
The Secretary	*The Big Easy*
Henry and June	*The Lover*
The Last Seduction	*White Palace*
Sea of Love	*The Hunger*
Last Tango in Paris	*9½ Weeks*
The Unbearable	*True Lies*
Lightness of Being	*Bella de Jour*
Lie with Me	*Eyes Wide Shut*
Chocolat	*Fabulous Baker Boys*
In the Realm of the Senses	*Blue Sky*

Here are a few other romantic film ideas provided by our road-test couples:

Top Gun	*Bull Durham*
Up in the Air	*Chasing Amy*
(500) Days of Summer	*Mr. and Mrs. Smith*
Don Juan De Marco	*Sleepless in Seattle*
Forgetting Sarah Marshall	*No Strings Attached*
Something's Gotta Give	*Desert Hearts*
An Officer and a Gentleman	*True Romance*

OPTION: A Candlelit Bath

Place candles around the bathtub before dinner, so your only post-dinner tasks are turning on the tap and lighting a match. The more candles, the better. We also recommend using your bubble bath, bath salts, or aromatic oils. Just settle into each other's arms and relax; if sex starts all over again, so be it, but it's not the point.

I undressed him in front of a mirror, taking my time with each button, touching his nipples under his cotton. I lingered over the belt and the zipper.

We combined our candlelit bath with dinner. We ate pad Thai-noodles right from the take-out container with chopsticks, in a nice, cozy candlelit tub. It was very decadent and indulgent!

We gave each other full-body massages and did food play. He dripped honey down my body, then slowly licked it all off.

To begin, partners can sit at opposite ends of a sofa, each with his or her foot in the other s lap. Massage each other's foot, experimenting with strokes and pressure, then tell each other how the rubbing and pressure points feel to you. Let your partner know what feels good and what doesn't. Wipe off excess oil so your feet won't be slippery.

When you are ready to move to the next stage, one partner finds a comfortable place to lie face down, while the other warms his or her hands and prepares to give a massage. Massage the back and shoulders; that's where most people hold the majority of their tension. Once that area is relaxed, move down to the buttocks and legs. After the person turns over, gently massage the neck and head, then work all the way down the front of the body to the feet. Remember, this massage is for pleasure, not for sexual arousal. Some people like their stomach massaged and others don't, so ask. That's a sensitive body part, so go easy and gentle.

For those who aren't accustomed to exchanging massages, start with a 10- to 15-minute massage, then switch roles—any longer and you risk losing out because your partner might fall asleep. Those accustomed to giving and getting massage know what they like and can take as long as they like.

> *We purchased scented oil that smelled like passion fruit and massaged each other with it. We alternated with our hands then used the "Magic Wand" in order to give each other a longer massage. It felt good to give that much.*

Putting More Play in Your Passion

For some of you, the evening may be over after dinner or the massages. But we've had road testers that were grateful that we offered more options so they could keep going.

OPTION: Adult (X-rated) Video

If you brought your laptop for online erotica, or have checked out the erotic movies that most hotels offer on demand, this is a good time to watch some adult entertainment.

My husband and I have been married for 15 years and I thought I knew him. I thought he would never agree to watch an X-rated movie and if he did, he'd be grossed out. I was shocked when he consented but even more surprised at how quickly he got excited. We watched about five minutes of the movie and then he was all over me—very, very hot. I'm sure we'll try this again.

Like the Sex Checks, the video can provide a way for couples to communicate without talking as they watch and respond to the film together. Or you can leave it on for its sounds of sex as background noise while you make love. If you're feeling in the mood, pretend the cameras are focused on you and your partner, and try to be sexier or naughtier than the porn stars.

We enjoyed watching a porno movie together because it seemed like we were having sex in the same room as those characters in the film.

Role-Playing Games

If you didn't engage in role-playing during dinner, you might want to play out a scenario now. Some fantasies are best acted out in private. If you do your own scene, or one suggested below, try to include sex acts or positions that your characters would want but that you would be reluctant to try in real life.

He blindfolded me during the foreplay. That intensified the feelings.

The Love Slave. You played poker—and lost. You bet everything on the last hand. At stake was your freedom, for one act of sexual pleasuring. And now you have to pay. You have to do *everything* the victor demands. The victor—secretly in love with the vanquished—makes sexual demands but ultimately wants the slave to end up craving more.

Here are some sexy scenarios our road-testers came up with:

> *We tried two. In the afternoon, we drove around the countryside. I played the role of a chauffeur; she was a French mistress. We never stepped out of those roles the entire afternoon. It was a gas! Sunday, my wife donned our daughter's old cheerleading outfit and we went from there.*

> *My husband was a pirate and I was a saucy lass posing as a cabin boy to get passage to Barbados (escaping a life of indentured servitude, of course). The pirate feels a strange attraction to the cabin boy (who tries hard to hide her gender!) and is quite relieved to find out she's a woman.*

OPTION: Body Painting

This can be a lot of fun. Many couples find it erotic to draw on each other's body. If this appeals to you, we hope you planned ahead and bought the nontoxic body paints described in Chapter 3. You may want to do this in the bathtub or shower. Take turns decorating each other's chest, breasts, back, buttocks, and genital area. Challenge yourself to integrate a specific body part into the scenery. The more imagination you use, the more fun it is. Plus, the brush strokes and wet paint feel quite sensuous on bare skin.

Washing each other off should be a slow, seductive experience. It might lead to sex in the bathtub or shower—which is the next option of the evening.

> *Take your own sheets if you go to a hotel. We trashed a set of sheets with chocolate and peanut butter and had to change them. I would have been mortified if this happened to the hotel's linens.*

OPTION: Sex Under Water

If you have sex in the bathtub, enjoy the feeling of the waves around your body and try not to flood the place! This is the time to use the silicone-based lubricants you brought with you because they last a lot longer in the water, and water will dry out a woman's vagina and can make intercourse painful. You don't want to have to end the weekend early because of soreness.

Or you might want to experiment with sex standing up in the shower. Making love with water streaming down your back in a hot steamy room can be both sensual and astoundingly erotic. Again, make sure you use a lot of lubricant in the shower, because the water may make penetration and thrusting more difficult.

OPTION: Hot and Cold Oral Sex

This is an exciting variation on the theme of prolonging your sexual experiences. Slowly lick, suck, and gently create a rhythm. After you have your partner very aroused, prepare to give (and receive) a real treat. Get some ice (small crescent-shaped cubes are best) and put it by the bedside. Put a small cube in your mouth for a few seconds, then remove it. Put your mouth on your partner's genitals quickly, while your mouth is still cold; your natural body temperature will make your mouth warm again, and your partner should love the alternating warm and cold feeling.

If you want to be truly exotic, bring a cup of hot tea to bed and swill some in your mouth before swallowing. Alternating ice and hot tea gives your partner the thrill of going from cold to hot and back again. You can become adept at holding the ice cube in your cheek and moving it to your lips, holding it there, then teasing the entire genital area. All of these variations on using hot and cold during oral sex can provide intense pleasure and unforgettable orgasm.

> *We decided to do this exercise blindfolded so each sensation would be a surprise.*

Another variation, if you like alternating sensations, is to use Trojan's Fire and Ice condoms whose dual action lubricant creates tingling sensations for both partners. If you dare, try the variety of Johnson and Johnson's KY jellies they named "Intense," an oil that when applied to the clitoris gives a strong warm tingling sensation.

OPTION: Tantric Sex

> *Gazing into her eyes and feeling the rhythm of our breathing took me beyond our bodies to a profound level of love.*

Tantric sex is the ancient sacred Hindu art of making love. We cannot do justice to this deep, intricate philosophy here, but the basic premise is to use focused breathing as a way to unify yourselves mentally, physically, and spiritually. By sharing tantric exercises with a partner, couples can reach a powerful emotional connection. Western culture typically separates sexuality from spirituality, and tantric exercises are a way to integrate them in a way that leads to a higher order of intimacy, sensuality, and orgasmic capacity.

You can have a great time exploring these exotic options even as a novice. Typically, couples face each other and synchronize their breathing. This exercise is a good way to slow down the pace of lovemaking and tune in to your partner. Try this position: Sitting naked, the male sits on the floor and the female sits on top of him, facing him with her legs over his, curling them around his waist for support; his legs can either be extended or curled around her buttocks. Each person places his or her right hand over the partner's heart. Maintaining eye contact, breathe slowly and deeply together for at least five minutes.

Breathing can also be used to intensify orgasm: About halfway into your climax, try drawing in your breath as slowly as possible; the intensity of your sensations will build for as long as you can sustain the inhalation. Then, when you have to exhale, let the air out in a noisy whoosh. Some tantric practitioners claim the more noise you make, the better your orgasm will feel. If you get really good at this, the orgasm can be extended with three or four additional exhalations!

If these exercises entice you to know more about tantric sex, you'll find much more detailed explanations in books like *Tantra: The Art of Conscious*

Living by Charles and Caroline Muir, or *The Heart of Tantric Sex: A Unique Guide to Love and Sexual Fulfillment* by Diana Richardson. Couples who incorporate tantra can enter a sexual meditation that has blissful results.

OPTION: Extending Your Orgasms

The goal of this exercise is to have mental control over your body in order to intensify sensation. Delaying orgasm as long as possible may well give you one of the most intense climaxes you have ever had. You probably won't get this right the first time you try, but the attempt will be fun.

Men: You will practice a form of discipline that trains you to get right up to the point of ejaculation and then stop, so that you learn to know when to save yourself for more stimulation. Sex therapists recommend withdrawal at the edge of ejaculation and the practice of the "squeeze technique"—which involves firmly squeezing the underside of the penis, where the head meets the shaft. A four-second squeeze to this part of the penis greatly diminishes the urge to ejaculate. Don't get upset if you misjudge how close you are; enjoy your orgasm and consider practicing this technique another time. If you are successful with this, you will probably feel a difference when you finally allow yourself to climax.

If you want to move on to the exotic level of this exercise, which includes learning to have multiple orgasms by separating orgasm from ejaculation, read *The Multi-Orgasmic Man* by Mantak Chia and Douglas Abrams Arava. Combining Western scientific knowledge with ancient Chinese sexual wisdom, the authors try to teach men how to have several whole-body orgasms without losing their erection, saving ejaculation until the final climax.

Women: Allow your partner to bring you to the brink but stopping short of orgasm. This can be done during either intercourse, touching, or oral sex. Give your partner a signal about how long you are really willing to hold off your climax. Try not to hurry your climax. When you are ready to have the world's most splendid orgasm, make sure you let your partner know so it doesn't accidentally get derailed by a change in tempo or withdrawal of stimulation. Communicate in a sexy whisper or shout "Don't stop," or "I'm ready to come."

Remember, the point is to stay on the edge of orgasm, as close as you can, for as long as you can. Of course, women are multi-orgasmic more frequently than men. Women may wish to come quickly, but let your partner know that on this special night you want seconds, thirds, or more!

THE NIGHT ENDS

We suspect that you're probably ready for a deep sleep.

> *Usually we move to our own sides of the bed to get a good night's rest, but Saturday we fell asleep in each other's arms. Being that close generated a warm glow that lasted all day Sunday.*

CHAPTER 6

Sunday Morning

Sunday mornings are the times to be lazy. So sleep in. Breakfast in bed is always a treat. Use room service, or if you prefer, go out to a little cafe and bring back warm muffins and gourmet coffee. Just enjoy the moment.

You may just be in the mood for cuddling now, but if you're up for one last sexual adventure of the weekend, we have some other playful options for you to try this morning.

> *My husband heated my towel in the dryer and presented it to me when I stepped out of the shower. He wanted to make the shower extra special, and he did.*

Now that your Sunday morning is off to a nice, slow start, you might be ready to choose your last sexy exercises for the weekend.

Exercise 1: Sex Toys

Even in the quiet early-morning hours, you may prefer something with bells, whistles, and batteries. For those of you who already know you like sex toys, try a new one. Or, if you bought your first sex toy as part of your preparation for your Great Sex Weekend, you and your partner will probably be comfortable and confident enough now to experiment.

I bought my girlfriend a vibrator with a G-Spot attachment as a surprise gift. First I gave her a full-body massage. Then we put on the G-Spot attachment up her bottom and we had sex. I could feel the vibrations—it was great! Later we laid it under her and I was in her, and again it was terrific. This was a first for both of us.

My boyfriend loved watching me reach multiple orgasms with my vibrator, because they are so intense. I never used one before, and it has really opened new doors to my sexuality.

EXERCISE 2: Talking Sexy

We think talking sexy can be incorporated into any of the exercises in this book. Once cultivated, this skill can help keep your sex life very lively indeed. You can get exactly what you want in bed, but *only* if you feel comfortable asking for it, and *only* if your partner feels comfortable about being told what you like.

We usually assume our partner can intuit our feelings so they don't have to be expressed. Yet few of us are mind readers. And even if we think we know how our partner feels, it's still a turn-on to *hear* the words. By simply stating aloud what is going on and how it makes you feel, you give your partner extreme pleasure and a sense of security. And this is very arousing.

My usually quiet lover turned into a very vocal man, describing in great detail what he was doing, what he was going to do, and then doing it. The sex talk was incredibly exciting and scintillating. We had the best sex ever. Slowly, deliberately, he narrated with a passion that was beyond belief.

Here are some sentiments that you might want to communicate to your partner:

Women:

♥ Compliments about his body or facial features

♥ How his hands feel on your body

♥ How you love the way his penis looks, how hard it is

♥ How much your are turned on when he enters or "fills" you

♥ How he feels inside you

♥ How it feels when he starts going fast/slow/gentle/ hard

♥ How much you love him

Men:

♥ How her skin feels

♥ Why you love her breasts

♥ How great it feels to hold her

- ♥ What you are thinking about when you first enter her

- ♥ How you feel when you're inside her

- ♥ How much you love her

We use sexier language while we're making love now. Having said those words once made it easier to use them again.

The Chinese Menu Game

In her book *Talk Sexy to the One You Love (and Drive Each Other Wild in Bed),* which we recommend to readers who want to go explore more verbal exercises, Barbara Keesling suggests writing out, then whispering, speaking aloud—even shouting— the words that complete these sentences: "I want to (<u>verb</u>) your (<u>noun</u>)" and "I want you to (<u>verb</u>) my (<u>noun</u>)."

We've taken Keesling's exercise a little farther by adding adjectives and adverbs, and suggest the following choices to spur you on. By all means, add your own words and phrases to the choices offered. Use them to complete these two sentences:

I want you to (<u>adverb</u>) (<u>verb</u>) my (<u>adjective</u>) (<u>noun</u>).

I want to (<u>adverb</u>) (<u>verb</u>) your (<u>adjective</u>) (<u>noun</u>).

ADVERBS	VERBS	ADJECTIVES	NOUNS
slowly	caress	beautiful	cock/penis
gently	nibble	sexy	balls
fast	suck	virile	breasts/tits
hard	tickle	hard	tummy
teasingly	fuck	sleek	bottom/butt
lightly	spank	taut	thighs
mercilessly	pull/tug	round	shoulders
lovingly	bite	strong	feet/toes
passionately	tease	soft	clitoris
sensuously	lick	hairy/hairless	G-spot
carefully	flick	color: pink,red	fingers
wildly	tongue	long	nipples
wickedly	play	juicy	chest
firmly	with	big	cunt/pussy
creatively	undress	delicious	vagina
powerfully	kiss	luscious	lips wet
calmly	eat/taste	lubricated	neck/throat

We loved talking dirty to each other. We've never done it before, and we found it quite arousing.

LAST SEX OF THE WEEKEND

The exercises you choose should lead to an exciting, open sexual experience. Whisper, talk, grunt, moan. Try something new, or something old but favored. Just keep sharing your thoughts and feelings during this last encounter before you get ready for lunch and the transition back to the real world.

CHAPTER 7

Sunday Afternoon: Perfect Endings

Her note read: "Remembering your sweetly scented skin, gentle coaxing hands, and tender murmurings of encouragement…"

The transitions from the weekend back to reality is as important as any other part of your getaway experience. Make this as gradual and unhurried as your best lovemaking.

It should be lunchtime about now. Check out of your hotel, but don't take off for home just yet. If you can, take time for one last meal somewhere calm and pleasant. Enjoy a leisurely lunch.

Here's an idea that may appeal to some of you. Take a minute to write just one or two sentences about the weekend, or about your feelings for your partner. Right before you go to bed, exchange your notes as the perfect ending for your weekend together.

I'm sorry that I don't tell you more often how attracted and in love I am with you. You are my man! You are my life!

I feel so alive when we are totally immersed sharing ourselves with each other, I love you.

He wrote, "Honey, I really didn't know how sexy you are capable of being until this weekend. I now look at you as my sex goddess."

LONG-TERM GAINS

After two kids and ten years of marriage, we'd slipped into a sexual rut. The book gave us an incentive to break our pattern. Now we're closer and more open to fun in bed than before.

The Great Sex Weekend is a way back to that kind of sharing. Sure, it is about sex and sensuality, but it is also about intimacy. And intimacy means opening up to each other, generously creating pleasure for each other, and remembering to be lovers who are full of curiosity about how to please and know each other better. This book can help remind you that if you give each other full attention for even just a weekend, and create a playful, amorous atmosphere, your sexual and emotional relationship can be rejuvenated. Once you've done that, the next challenge is to not let the spirit and excitement of this weekend fade away. Now you have the tools to infuse the reality of your everyday lives with the pleasures and insights of these past two days.

I wish we could do this every weekend! (All week, too!) I wish I could always have all the time in the world to devote to my marriage, but unfortunately, the more mundane (and less important) parts of my life tend to take over. Our next getaway—on our anniversary—won't come soon enough!

CHAPTER 8

Making Love in Everyday Life

We hope this time-out for sex and intimacy has encouraged you to feel really good about yourself and your relationship. This is a good time to think about your sex life and love life and what you gained from your weekend experience that you'd like to carry into everyday life.

Take an assessment of your usual lovemaking schedule. How often do you have sex (honestly)? There is no "right" answer. The frequency of sex for ALL couples diminishes significantly after the first year of a relationship and then decreases slowly over time. On average a couple may, depending in large part on age, have sex one to three times a week. In older relationships, a couple might be happy having sex as infrequently as once a month.

Review the last month before you started preparations for your sexy getaway. If the frequency was average for you, is that the amount of sex you or your partner want to have? If so, frequency is not a problem. However, if either of you feels that you make love too infrequently, discuss what would be a realistic amount of sex that would please you both. If you have different appetites, you might have to arrive at a compromise.

Do you often make love late at night, after 11 P.M., when you're both really too tired for a quality experience? When would be the perfect time?

89

Sunday mornings? If you don't like sex in the morning, would you like to have sex on a weekend afternoon? If so, does that ever happen anymore? If you like having sex at night, is there some way you can both turn in early on nights when you're feeling amorous (or, at least, horny)? Should you turn off the TV earlier, or set the alarm ahead half an hour for more morning time together? Now that you've spent this luxurious time experimenting, how has it reminded you of the best ways to stage your sex life to maximize your energy and concentration?

Does each of you initiate sex enough? Does your partner wish you initiated sex more often, or vice versa? If not, try to replay the role reversal exercise, at least once a month.

Do you both set aside enough time for an occasional candlelit dinner at a restaurant or at home with the phones turned off? Many people think that such occasions should arise naturally and spontaneously. And sometimes they do. But they happen more often when couples are honest enough to admit that they need to take the time and make the effort to keep their romance vibrant.

> *My husband is taking more time kissing me than he did he-fore this weekend.*

> *We've done a lot more fantasy role-flaying since the weekend. It's a great part of our sex life now.*

After 11 years, we were like other couples who have lived together that long. We were way too busy and a little angry at the ways we took each other for granted. Instead of continuing to blame the other person, this book made us realize our problem was pretty common in these times. And we still make "dates" to be with each other, which we didn't do before.

OLD HOUSES, NEW PLACES

Finally, look around your home. **Are there places where you've never made love?** The kitchen floor? Your desk? In front of the fireplace? On top of the dryer? Your kids' swing set? Get playful. Use your imagination and have some outrageous fun.

She sat on the counter in the bathroom and we made love, watching our reflections in the mirror.

An Invitation to Our Readers

We'd love to know what you liked the best about your first getaway and what you look forward to in your future sex getaways. Consider writing a blog entry at our website: **www.thegreatsexweekend.com**

This comment is our favorite, so far:

This book is like battery cables. Everyone should have it handy to jump-start their love life!

APPENDIX 1

When You Can't Get Away:
Doing the Weekend at Home

*We both did the preparation, which was minor.
We decided to stay at home and already had
most of the stuff we would need.*

If you decide not to travel for whatever reason,
you can modify the home setting to ready it for the
weekend:

If you can afford it—or need new sheets
anyhow—we recommend buying new linen for the
occasion. You can go with tasteful designs for
everyday use, or try inexpensive satiny sheets for how
differently they feel on this—and future—sexy
weekends. On the other hand, if you worry about
stains, you might prefer to put old sheets on the bed.
You might even buy a cheap shower curtain or stop at
a paint or hardware store and get an inexpensive
plastic tarp if you're thinking of trying the body
paints. At the very least, use fresh sheets for the
weekend.

> *We love flannel sheets to keep cozy in the
> winter. A soft cotton throw rug works well for
> juicy sex.*

> *I bought inexpensive Indian print fabric and
> draped it over the bed. We pretended we were
> in a Persian palace!*

We bought a cheap shower curtain and put it on the floor. We drizzled about a half a cup of vegetable oil and one half cup of warm water over it. We started with back rubs and slipped and slided into sex.

Lighting is important. Bright, glaring light can make you feel inhibited. A soft, flattering light helps both men and women feel sexy. We sought advice from Marsha Hunt, award-winning writer-producer for *Playboy* Home Videos: "Blue light bulbs create an atmosphere that is mysterious and sensual. We always use blue light in our bedroom scenes. It gives enough light to see, but it's dark enough to cover flaws, too. Pink bulbs provide light that is very soft, romantic, and flattering (it makes most people look much younger), but stick to a 40-watt bulb if you use pink. Stay away from green—that's monster lighting—and yellow, which makes skin look sallow." We suggest that you stay away from red bulbs, too, because they make the bedroom look like a brothel. You can find blue and pink bulbs at any well-stocked hardware or large discount store.

We decided not to follow your advice and used green light-bulbs, because green is our favorite color and they really helped us feel comfortable and sexy.

I changed our bedside light to pink. It gave the room a soft, romantic feel.

Our road-testers convinced us that the 1960s are fondly remembered—even by those too young to have been a part of the era.

We always find our black light sets a romantic mood; we burn incense too.

We use a blue lava lamp when we make love.

Nothing is as romantic as firelight, so if you have a fireplace, be sure to stock up on firewood. Find a big old comforter to place in front of the fireplace. The delicious smell of wood burning pleases the senses, and you'll have perfect, flickering light for lovemaking.

We hadn't used our fireplace in three years. We spent the entire night in front of it. We had dinner by firelight, and that's where we gave each other our massages. It was incredibly romantic.

We recommend lots of drip-less candles— scented if you enjoy that; unscented if scents are distracting. If you have lots of candleholders, pick up a few packages of candles. If you don't have candlesticks, you'll find inexpensive votive candles in glass holders at stores like Pier 1, Target, bath or beauty supply stores, and drugstores; buy at least eight. If you have the space, surround your bathtub with 20 of those short, flat tea lights, the kind packaged in round tins.

QUICK TIP #1: Place all candles on fireproof surfaces, away from drafts. Never leave any candle unattended.

Flowers are always wonderful; they add fragrance, color, and sensual shapes to a room. Especially if you don't usually buy them, flowers announce that it is a special weekend. Buy a bouquet for your dining table or just a stem or two for a bud vase on the nightstand.

I sent flowers to his office as a way to say "I love you." He brought them home for us to enjoy for the weekend.

These were my favorites for the room: freesia, Casablanca lilies, and orange blossoms.

Music is an important part of setting a romantic mood. We assume you have a docking station for your iPod or other mobile music system that you can use in both the bedroom and dining room. Select music that you know you both will enjoy. For this special weekend, try to vary the music you make love to. Sex is different with different kinds of music. For example, if you usually listen to soft mood music, try some light rock 'n' roll. Keeping up with a faster beat can be a lot of fun. If you usually have sex without music, adding music will enhance the experience.

Making love to Kitaro, a Japanese New Age artist, is great because there are no words to distract us and the beautiful melodies intensify and prolong our passion.

We started out dancing to Melissa Etheridge but moved to the sofa pretty quickly. Making love to really loud music with a powerful beat is good clean, aerobic fun.

<u>Preparing Your Home for Romance</u>. If your home is not always squeaky clean and free of clutter, invest the time or money for this occasion. Bathtubs, in particular, must look inviting. Reminders of work or house projects should be kept out of sight. If you normally keep lots of pictures of the kids or other family

members on the dresser across from your bed, we suggest that you put them away—or at least facedown— so their images don't interfere with the spirit of carefree romance or lust.

Doing the program in their own home was just right for some road-testers:

We love being at home, and we did a lot to make it special. We put the stereo in our bedroom. I added strings of whimsical lights (we picked out fun and cheap ones from the Lillian Vernon catalog). Little Christmas lights would work, too. I also put lots of flowers everywhere.

Staying at home was great, easy, and we didn't have to spend a lot of money. Friday night we had great finger foods—shrimp cocktail, pot stickers, fried stuffed mushrooms, roasted red pepper and garlic cheese spread on great bread with a good bottle of wine. The next night we got a gourmet pizza delivered.

GUARDING YOUR PRIVACY

It is essential to feel that neither your mood nor your activities will be interrupted. Agree to turn off the ringer on *all* phones for the weekend. If you need to check on the children, elderly parents, or the office via phone, text, or e- mail, set aside one or two specific times during the weekend to make contact with the outside world, and don't violate that schedule.

It's difficult for people with children or other continuous responsibilities to relax unless they know they can be reached for emergencies. We recommend you figure out a way to be "on call" for children or other emergencies, but unreachable by others. For example, arrange with a trusted neighbor to be your go-between. The neighbor can ring your bell if you are needed. Lots of road-testers told friends and family that they'd be out of town when in fact they stayed at home.

A *note on pet care:* Obviously, if you're doing this program at home, you've resolved your childcare arrangements. Several at-home road-testers were surprised by how much their pets detracted from their weekend hideaway. They all offered the same solution: "Kennel your pets!" If you don't, at least keep them out of the bedroom.

Home Court Advantage

> *After our walk, we went home and opened our wedding album from 14 years ago. We hadn't looked at these for a long time. It made us feel very close.*

If you're having dinner at home, make it a treat. Put out your best china and glasses and, if you have a small table that can be moved easily, consider dining in front of the fireplace, or on a balcony or porch. If you prefer being more casual, have a picnic with fancy paper plates in front of the fireplace or in the backyard.

> *We grilled chicken outside in the middle of a snowstorm and then came inside and cuddled by the fire. It was very romantic.*

*I roasted a bulb of garlic and with my fingers
smeared it on thin slices of a sweet baguette
with herb brie cheese and a touch of mango
chutney, and fed it to her.*

If you're at home, breakfast can be both
luxurious and simple—perhaps croissants with a
poached egg on a pretty plate, or just warm scones,
coffee, and juice. You can make a half melon more
tempting by filling it with ripe berries. Unless cooking
is part of foreplay for you, don't interrupt the flow of
the morning by having to spend too much time in the
kitchen.

*The program did a wonderful thing for us: It
allowed us to reclaim our home as a safe
heaven. Life is so busy that we had become
very task-oriented and forgotten how to rest.
It's okay to waste time at home. Two Sundays
after our "sex holiday," we watched a golf
tournament, made love in the afternoon, and
then took a nap together. Our home is a wonderful place again.*

APPENDIX 2

A 24-Hour Plan

The 24-Hour Plan was really perfect for us. I think most people with two jobs and two kids don't really get much more time than this.

We recognized that some couples need an abbreviated plan if they are to participate at all. For them, we have included two different one-day plans. We've highlighted some of the exercises and activities from the weekend getaway that we think will be most beneficial to couples who want to jump-start their sex lives in a very short time.

PLAN ONE: SATURDAY MORNING UNTIL SUNDAY MORNING

The first short program is intended for those who are staying at home and devoting a full Saturday to each other. Here we provide only the rudimentary outline of the plan and include reference to pages in previous chapters that offer more detail.

BREAKFAST IN BED. This luxury is the earliest and easiest way to signal that today is special. Take turns pampering each other; one partner prepares breakfast in bed on Saturday, the other on Sunday. (See ch. 4 for specific suggestions.)

BATHING TOGETHER. Take a sensual shower or bath together. (See ch. 4 for playful bathing ideas.)

EXCHANGING FULL BODY MASSAGES. While you're in the mood to spoil your partner and be spoiled yourself, we recommend that you consult ch. 5 to learn about how to relax and enjoy the intimacy of swapping massages. We also suggest trying the pleasuring exercises (described in ch.3`), which will show you how to incorporate giving and getting feedback into your massage experience. Like pleasuring, massage helps you rediscover the full range of erotic stimulation, but it is also an occasion to communicate with each other how you are feeling and how you want to be touched.

ROLE-REVERSAL TIME. By reversing many of the traditional male and female roles, women can more readily become the sexual initiator. Among other suggestions, we encourage women to select new, exciting positions for intercourse. Four positions are described in ch.4, along with some tips for making the Sadie Hawkins concept work for you.

AFTERNOON BREAK. We don't expect or recommend that you stay in bed all day. Instead of the all-afternoon break described in chapter 4, a two-hour break fits this plan better. Some of the suggested activities listed there are suitable, or you can simply take a leisurely walk or drive. Weather permitting, pack a picnic lunch and head to a relaxing outdoor setting. A long lunch at a restaurant with a beautiful view is a good second choice.

TOUCHING OR ORAL SEX TO CLIMAX. The "his and her" exercises described in ch.3 remind you that

all sex doesn't have to be centered around intercourse. You can bring each other to an exciting
orgasm with your hands and mouth.

ROLE PLAYING AT DINNER. If you think it
would be enjoyable, step out of your own lives and into a
sexy, romantic "play" at dinner where you each take the
lead roles. See ch.5 for ideas and cautionary notes.

ALTERNATE DINNER EXERCISE- INTIMATE
TALK. In ch.3 and ch.6, you'll find suggestions for
romantic and sexy topics that will tease and tantalize.
You may never make it to dessert.

SEX ON A SATURDAY NIGHT. For those of
you who engaged in fantasy role-playing at dinner, stay
in character. Sex automatically takes on a fresh and
different flavor when you're pretending to be someone.
Your post-dinner lovemaking can be very exciting.

If you didn't indulge in a fantasy scenario, you
may prefer to try out a new sex toy (see ch.6), swap
fantasies (ch.5) or sex checks (see ch.2), paint each
other's body or watch an adult video (see ch.5). Any
of these props should also lead you to out-of-the
ordinary sexual fun.

RELAX WITH A ROMANTIC MOVIE. It's nice to
relax and snuggle after sex. Pick a light romantic
comedy or drama that you enjoyed together in the past
but haven't seen in years. For those who'd like to try
something a little sexier, go for an R-rated film (see
ch.5).

SUNDAY MORNING. This is the last breakfast in bed, or brunch on the patio, before reentry to everyday life. Take a few minutes to write one or two sentences about your Saturday together, or about your feelings for your partner, and exchange your notes. Or you might discuss what you'd like to do on your next sex weekend, especially places you'd love to stage your getaway.

PLAN TWO: SATURDAY AFTERNOON TO SUNDAY AFTERNOON

The second short program is intended for those who can get away from home. It conforms to most late-afternoon check-in and noon checkout times. Here we offer a rudimentary outline of the plan and reference to pages in previous chapters that offer more detail.

AN INTIMATE LUNCH. You can request early check-in privileges, but we're assuming you'll have to wait until after lunch to get into most hotels. When you reach your destination, have lunch in the prettiest restaurant on the premises or in the nearby vicinity. Consult the list of suggested romantic or sexy conversation topics described in ch.3 and ch.6 that will put you in the mood for the twenty-four hours ahead.

AFTERNOON NOOKY. Following your intimate lunch, you probably can't wait to get to your room. We recommend that you carefully read about the post-dinner activities described in ch.6. For the afternoon adaptation, start by undressing each other (this can be slow and teasing or fast and desperate) and doing the kissing exercise. Skip the pleasuring exercise and move directly to the eye-contact exercise, which involves touching, looking, and talking. From there, as you'll see, you are encouraged to pleasure each other with some combination of touching, oral and even anal stimulation, as well as intercourse to orgasm, as you like it.

BATHING TOGETHER. After sex, take a sensual shower or bath together. See ch.4 for suggestions. If it's already getting dark, you might consider taking a candlelit bath. See ch.5 for ideas about how to enhance your bath. If the hotel has a Jacuzzi, this might be a nice time to enjoy that relaxing activity together.

SHORT WALK AND TALK. This is an easy activity to do just about anywhere you go, but if you feel the need for more exercise, see what the hotel or area offers. You don't need to indulge in a full workout. The important thing is to be together.

COCKTAILS, DINNER, AND FANTASY. If you think it would be enjoyable, we recommend stepping out of your own lives and into a sexy, romantic "play" for pre-dinner cocktails. This role-playing should carry you through dinner. Read ch.5 for ideas and cautionary notes. A "pickup" or "first meeting" scene is the easiest to enact in a public place.

RELAX WITH AN IN-ROOM MOVIE. Select a sexy drama or a romantic comedy. Relax and snuggle or have more sex. This should be a low-key prelude to a long, deep sleep together.

BREAKFAST IN BED. Call for room service and indulge yourselves in this out-of-the-ordinary luxury.

ROLE REVERSAL TIME. A little role reversal can bring added excitement to any relationship, so we encourage the woman to take on the role of sexual initiator (see ch.4). We suggest that she select positions for intercourse that she has never explored before. Four positions are described in ch.4.

LAST STROLL OR LUNCH. Before you return to everyday life, write each other a brief one or two sentence note about the highlights of your mini-getaway. Include feelings about your relationship and your partner (see ch.7). Exchange and talk about your notes. If you want to go further, you can have a conversation based on the questions posed in ch.8 that can help you improve your everyday erotic life. You might include what you'd like to do on your next getaway.

> *We had too much anxiety about getting away for two days. One day was perfect. No guilt. No regrets. We think we should do the one-day getaway at least once a month.*

APPENDIX 3

The Week-Long Sex Getaway

I chose a beach resort for our first getaway, so my girlfriend picked a quiet mountain resort with very private cabins surrounded by redwoods for a completely different feel for our next one.

SPECIAL VACATIONS

Don't forget that a new location can make repeating the same getaway feel totally different. If you had a fabulous experience the first time, try to imagine it taking place in Puerto Vallarta, the Bahamas, or somewhere else you've always wanted to see. All these locations have something to offer—each one will bring out a different aspect of the experience.

We recognize some couples can get away for longer than a weekend, so here expand ideas for your luxuriously long time together. This allows us to suggest additional places, including some exotic international destinations at the very end of our Appendix on "Getaway Places."

Have fun thinking about what you would like to do on this special getaway. Where would you like to go when you can go away for at least a week? Because you'll have more time, we offer you some more suggestions that might have appeal for both of you. This is a great opportunity for a little more exploration and innovation.

Option 1: Taking It Off

Start one of your lovemaking sessions as a striptease artist. Each partner can do this on a separate night as a "show" for the other; having a couple of drinks helps loosen inhibitions. This is one of those occasions when a red light bulb creates just the right effect. Dress in sexy underwear.

Women can buy a see-through body suit or bra. Put on whatever music you like—hard rock or rhythm and blues is nice background for this game. The partner who is doing the striptease will get excited by acting out this fantasy role.

Men, you can wear bikini underwear under your shorts, or strip down to your shorts and stroke yourself so that your partner sees your erection while you're dancing. If dancing is embarrassing for either of you, just walk around seductively to the music. You'll be amazed at how erotic this can be.

If you're really motivated, check out clips like "How to Perform a Striptease" on YouTube. Free education!

Option 2: Touching and Other Good Vibrations

Vibrators can vary greatly in length and diameter. Check out what is comfortable. The vibrator can be used gently on the penis and in or around the anal area. For women, use one on the outside, near the clitoris, and the other inside the vagina or anus. *Partners sharing sex toys should thoroughly wash them, and always wash toys after using them near the anus.* Used gently and with a lot of feedback from your partner about what feels good, these sex aids can definitely drive both men and women wild.

Option 3: So Many Positions

It's time for a few more acrobatic positions. This is a good time to sit down with the books you bought like *The Joy of Sex* and see what appeals to you.

Here are some of our ideas for less common positions. Try one where you're both standing, with him behind her or one where she is lying on the bed and he is standing over her.

Have him lay on his back and her mount while on her knees, facing away from.

Or partners can both be on their knees on the floor, her knees on top of his as she balances with her feet.

Invent new ways to enter and be entered; every angle is a new sensation. We've added a few more illustrations to spark your imagination.

"69" is a challenging position for oral sex. This position aligns you facing each genital area,

with the goal of sucking and licking each other at the same time. There are two variations: In the first, one partner lies on his or her back and the other person is on top; in the second, they lie side by side. If one partner reaches orgasm only on his or her back, obviously the first position is better, and that person should be the "bottom" of the couple.

The advantage is simultaneous arousal; the disadvantage is losing your concentration on the other person as your own excitement becomes overwhelming. You may want to be pleasure-oriented rather than orgasm-driven in this position. Reaching orgasm can be difficult, but it is wonderful when it happens. You can move back to intercourse, or some other activity, when you feel ready to have an orgasm.

Option 4: Don't Do This One If…You're Going to Run for Public Office

One of the sexiest things you can do is make love in an unusual place outside the home- on a beach or in an unlit pool in the summer or in hot springs in the middle of winter. Go camping and put up a tent; rain or shine, there's something really special in making love outside.

The awareness that you might be seen is one factor that makes sex in public places really hot, but be sure that you don't put yourself in any danger or risk of being arrested for lewd and lascivious behavior.

Option 5: Light bondage and discipline

We decided to experiment with ß&D on this getaway. Using thigh-high nylons as impromptu restraints was totally sexy.

It's not easy (or necessary) to explain why restraints are so sexy for some people, or why imposing your will or submitting to your partners is such a turn-on. Being "ravished"—well, by the ravisher of your choice—can be thrilling. When playing this game, be sure to take turns. A lot of men like being tied up and ravished, too. You can flip a coin to decide which roles to play—the ravisher or the ravished. Before you start, agree on how long this activity will last. You both need to understand and agree that if either partner gets uncomfortable and says "Stop!" the game ends.

The following scenario is a good beginning: Pretend that the ravisher has been granted three wishes that cannot be refused. Let s say that you've chosen the role of ravisher. Your first wish is that you get to tie up your partner. You can do this with silk scarves, or you can use leather handcuffs.

If you want to make sure no one gets bruised, use soft, fleece-lined Velcro cuffs. Remember, this is just play; no one should get hurt. The person who is being tied up and is submitting to the other's wishes really controls the action. This game has got to be consensual; otherwise, it's abusive.

What are your other two wishes? Do you want to sexually "torture" your victim by turning him on and denying any orgasm until he begs for it? Do you want to leave one hand free, then "order" your partner to masturbate to climax? Or, if she's the slave, you may want her to lie face down and enter her from behind.

Maybe while your partner is positioned rump up and very turned on, you can start lightly spanking, if you know for sure she or he would think it's fun. Try just one light smack, and see what the response is. If your partner gives clear feedback that this is exciting, you can slap again. Gradually increase intensity with the flat of your hand on the lower buttocks. The partner being spanked tells the other when it's hard enough and when to stop. If this is new territory for you, take it slowly and be sure your partner consents enthusiastically—otherwise, stop.

In such "dominance" play, you want to get in touch with pleasing by controlling. In fact, you're allowing your partner to be wildly absorbed in his or her own pleasure. When you're the one being tied up, you're being ordered to do sexual things. You bear no responsibility. Being controlled can be a source of freedom and excitement.

Of course, this kind of experimentation requires a lot of trust. Don't try these games if you are not absolutely sure that bondage and discipline can be safe and non-threatening for both of you.

Option 6: Gender-Bending

Have you ever wanted to pretend you are a member of the opposite sex? This idea might disgust you—or intrigue you. If the latter is true, go for it. If you are a woman, pretend making love as if you were a man—how *you* think it should be done. If you are a man, keep a little role reversal in your mind—it could be a great turn on and a lot of fun.

APPENDIX 4

FOR SEXY FUN: A LIST OF USEFUL WEBSITES

The websites listed here were selected because they guarantee to be discreet and protect your privacy. Items and packages are sent in plain wrappers. All promise to never sell, rent, or trade your name to another business or organization. It's always a good idea to review the company privacy policy yourself to maximize your comfort level.

For specialty shopping, go to:

GOOD VIBRATIONS- *www.goodvibes.com*
PHONE: 1-800-BUY VIBE 8 A.M.-6 P.M. PACIFIC TIME.
Especially good for vibrators and literary and visual erotica that appeals to women.

XANDRIA COLLECTION *www.xandria.com*
PHONE: 1-800-242-2823 7 A.M.-5 P.M. PACIFIC TIME

BABELAND: SEX TOYS FOR A PASSIONATE WORLD *www.babeland.com*
PHONE: 1-800-658-9119 9 A.M. TO 5 P.M. PACIFIC TIME

EVE'S GARDEN- *www.evesgarden.com*
PHONE: 1-800-848-3837 11 A.M. TO 7 P.M.
EASTERN TIME

LOVERS-PACKAGE YOUR Passion
www.loverspackage.com

HANKY PANKY AFTER MIDNIGHT
www.hankypanky.com
PHONE: 1.877.447.4811, 9 A.M. to 6 P.M.
EASTERN TIME
Especially good for lingerie

TROJAN *www.trojancondoms.com*
Check out their new "Fire and Ice" lubricated
condoms that deliver both warming and tingling
sensations to both partners.

Visit **www.thegreatsexweekend.com** to read
about newest products we discover and where
to get them....or to blog and share YOUR
product "discoveries" for a great sex weekend
with other readers.

APPENDIX 5

Getaway Places
in the U.S.A. and Canada

This is not an exhaustive list of cities or hotels, just some ideas of places we like and think you might like too. Some hotels were suggested by road-test couples; others are ones that we personally have known and loved. Some hotels and inns have offered discounts, little gifts, or extra services to couples doing our program; we suggest that you mention our book in those places.

It's hard to rate hotels according to price—everyone has a different notion of what is considered expensive. Also, certain cities operate on a different scale. For example, what is reasonable in New York City is considered expensive almost everywhere else. So here is our general approach: If a room is under $140, or close to it, we call it inexpensive. If it is between $140 and $250, we call it moderate. If it is over $250, we say it is expensive.

National Hotel Chains: In addition to the city-by-city list that follows, check their websites for specials. The major hotel chains offer "romance packages" subject to availability (there is some variation according to individual hotel). For example, Marriott sometimes offers "Weekends for Two," with free breakfast in bed, 25 percent off dinner, and late Sunday checkout. Call 800-USA-WKND. Hilton's "Romance Package" typically includes breakfast, a bottle of champagne or sparkling cider, bubble bath, and chocolate-covered strawberries. Call 800-HILTONS. Hyatt's "Romance Packages" are less generous, but call 800-233-1234 and inquire about details.

For more of our featured destinations, please visit us:
www.thegreatsexweekend.com
and
www.hisandhervacations.com

UNITED STATES

Atlanta

THE RITZ CARLTON, BUCKHEAD-
www.ritzcarlton.com 3434 Peachtree Road N.E. (404) 237-2700. This hotel doesn't look like the classic Ritz Carlton from the outside, but inside it is all paneling and flowers and oil paintings. The good news is that it's a better price than most and includes all their usual amenities, like terrific service and a good health club. There is a very fancy, romantic restaurant and a great open bar for people watching. The rooms are romantic, and when you take your break, there are some great shopping plazas right across the street. Moderate to expensive.

GRAND HYATT-
www.grandatlanta.hyatt.com 3300 Peachtree Road. (404)237-1234. If you like the elegance of simple but luxurious Japanese ambience, this is the

place for you. There are beautiful Japanese gardens to stroll through and rooms that are tasteful and spacious. We like the attention to details: marble bathrooms with thick terry robes, 24-hour room service, and fine service. Moderate to expensive.

CHATEAU ELAN-
www.chateauelan.com 100 Rue Charlemagne, Braselton. 800-233-WINE (9463). This is a large resort with a spa, golf course, tennis courts, and riding facilities. The European ambience includes a very serious approach to food. We recommend it because many of the suites have been built to house honeymooners. The rooms vary widely; in fact, this hotel has been known to carry low price specials for lovers, such as the hot date package. Be sure to ask if this hotel is offering any romantic getaway packages. Moderate.

Boston

THE RITZ-CARLTON, BOSTON COMMON-
www.ritzcalton.com 10 Avery Street. (617) 574-7100. This is one of the nicest hotels in the whole chain. Want to be pampered? Want to feel special? Look no further. The French public rooms are exquisite, and your room is likely to be lovely, too. There is limousine service upon request—in fact, you ask, and they deliver. Not surprisingly, expensive.

BOSTON HARBOR HOTEL, ROWES WHARF-
www.bhh.com 70 Rowes Wharf. (617) 439-7000. What a wonderful place to get away to. This hotel has large bedrooms with large baths, and the public rooms

feel celebratory. For a break, there is a spa and indoor pool, and at night their lounge offers good jazz. Moderate to expensive.

THE NEWBURY GUEST HOUSE-
www.newburyguesthouse.com 14 Embankment Road, Beacon Hill. (800) 437-7668. This is Victorian Boston, a four-story town house built in 1882. Some people think it's Boston's best lodging—at any price. There is a wonderfully cozy atmosphere and a great location. Inexpensive to moderate.

MILLENNIUM BOSTONIAN HOTEL BOSTON-
www.millenniumhotels.com 26 North Street at Faneuil Hall Market Place. (617) 523-360. This place feels like a small urban inn, even though it has 152 rooms. There are balconies and French doors and French furniture, all of which add up to a very romantic atmosphere. Some of the rooms have fireplaces; all have VCRs, oversize bathtubs, and terry robes. Moderate to expensive.

... *NEAR BOSTON*

Cambridge

THE CHARLES HOTEL-
www.charleshotel.com One Bennett Street. (617) 864-1200. This is a charming medium-size hotel with inviting rooms that tell you are in New England. We especially like the quilted down comforters. There is 24-hour room service and a health club and spa. Moderate to expensive.

Martha's Vineyard

THE CAPTAIN R. FLANDER'S HOUSE-
www.captainflandersinn.com 440 North Road,
Chilmark, MA. (508) 645-3123. This is a lovely bed-
and-breakfast in a historic house on lovely acreage
overlooking Bliss Pond. This B&B reeks Martha
Stewart—in fact, she featured it in one of her books. It
is small. The best place for lovers is the separate
cottage with fireplace. Very romantic. By the way, they
host weddings. Moderate.

OUTERMOST INN-
www.outermostinn.com. 81 Lighthouse Road,
Aquinnah, MA. (508) 645-3511. If your idea of
romance is a classic Vineyard shingled house on a bluff
overlooking the sea, search no more. There is a first-rate
restaurant, lovely rooms (including one suite), and
simple romantic decoration. Expensive.

THORNCROFT INN-
www.thorncroft.com 460 Main Street, Vineyard
Haven, MA. (508) 693-3333 More laid-back than
some of the others. You can stay in the main inn or in
a remodeled carriage house. Less family oriented, so
better for lovers—especially the private hot tubs, which
can be reserved, or request one of their rooms with
two person whirlpools. Moderate.

Central California Coast

SYCAMORE MINERAL SPRINGS RESORT-
www.sycamoresprings.com 1215 Avila Beach Drive,
San Luis Obispo. (800) 234-5831. This is a natural

hot springs resort located on a hillside, only three minutes from the beach. Each room features a full-size spa and private balcony; suites have fireplaces, oversize showers, and four-poster beds. Other spa amenities offered. Romantic restaurant on premises. Mention our book. Moderate to expensive.

RIPPLEWOOD INN-
www.ripplewoodresort.com 47047 Route 1, Big Sur. (408) 667-2242. Individual heated redwood cabins, most with kitchens and fireplaces. Some have two bedrooms and private decks. Inexpensive.

THE MADDONA INN-
www.madonnainn.com 100 Madonna Road, San Luis Obispo. (800) 543-9666. 109 different rooms, ranging from one with seven-foot bathtub, another has a cave room theme with a waterfall shower, then there's a hearts-and-flowers for the truly sentimental. This is only for couples with a sense of humor. Be prepared for hordes of tourists; this place is kitschy fun. Moderate.

LA BELLASERA HOTELS AND SUITES-
www.labellasera.com 206 Alexa Court, Paso Robles (805) 238-2834. 60 large luxury oversized rooms and suites, signature bedding and in-room spa treatments make this Mediterranean-style boutique resort, nestled in the heart of Paso Robles wine country, a find. They pride themselves on service. Moderate.

ANN HARPER'S BED AND BREAKFAST-
www.annharpersbedandbreakfast.com 56 Smith
Street. (843) 723-3947. This is the real thing—by the
time you leave, you'll understand what "southern
hospitality" means. Ann Harper gives her guests one
of the city's few remaining full homemade Southern
breakfasts as well as personal attention to help them
discover the "hidden Charleston."

CHARLESTON PLACE HOTEL-
www.charlestonplace.com 205 Meeting Street. (888)
635-2350. If you prefer the privacy of hotels and
money is no object, stay at the Charleston Place Hotel,
one of the world-famous Orient-Express luxury hotels,
which also houses the Charleston Grill with its rare
four-star rating from Mobil. Splurge on The Romance
Getaway Package with exclusive accommodations,
French champagne and a dozen roses. Expensive.

27 STATE STREET BED AND BREAKFAST-
www.charleston-bb.com 27 State Street. (843) 722-
4243. Built in 1800 in the French Quarter, this old
private residence now has suites with private entrances,
some with fireplaces and kitchens. Flowers and fruit
in the room. Beach close by. Inexpensive to moderate.

MIDDLETON INN-
www.theinnatmiddletonplace.com 4290 Ashley
River Road. (800) 543-4774. On a fabulous old
plantation. Play Rhett and Scarlett. Great grounds
for holding hands and romance. Lovely, classic
furnishings. Privacy. Moderate to expensive.
JOHN RUTLEDGE HOUSE-

www.johnrutledgehouse.com 116 Broad Street.
(800) 476-9741. Antebellum mansion on the Historic
Register. An old ballroom with wrought-iron staircases
is locale for tea and sherry in the afternoon. Poster beds
and lavish baths, two with Jacuzzis. Marble fireplaces
in some rooms. Inexpensive to moderate.

THOMAS LAMBOLL HOUSE-
www.lambollhouse.com 19 King Street. (888) 874-
0793. This is an antebellum masterpiece (built in 1739)
just off the Battery in the heart of the historic district
that has just two guest rooms with French doors
leading to the piazza. Inexpensive (depending on
season).

Chicago

THE DRAKE-
www.thedrakehotel.com 140 East Walton Place.
(800) 553-7253. This is a Chicago institution, and it
looks a little bit like a place where ladies lunch. But
you are right across from a wonderful beach and can
turn the corner to some of the best walking/shopping
streets in the world. If you get a room with a water view,
it can be spectacular. As with other older, venerable
hotels you have to request a good room that's big
enough. A lot of class, and service. Moderate to
expensive.

SUTTON PLACE HOTEL-
www.chicago.suttonplace.com 21 East Bellevue
Place. (866) 3SUTTON. This is right in the center of
the Gold Coast near Lake Michigan, and it is a handsome place. There is art deco decoration and big

rooms with great sound systems. The bathrooms are a special plus; they are large, and each one has a soaking tub with a separate shower. Twenty-four-hour room service, of course. Moderate to expensive.

THE FOUR SEASONS HOTEL-
www.preview.fourseasons.com 120 East Delaware Place. (312) 280-8800. If you want a splurge getaway, do it here. The lobby is on the seventh floor, and when you walk in you feel as if you are in an especially luxurious place. The rooms with a view of the skyline or Lake Michigan are terrific. Expensive.

THE TALBOTT-
https://talbotthotel.reachlocal.net 20 East Delaware. (888) 821-2256. This is a real find on the Gold Coast. Based on the personal approach of a European hotel, this hotel specializes in romance and offers Suite Dreams Weekends, which feature champagne, flowers, and a one-bedroom suite and Sunday brunch. Paneled public rooms with fireplaces and room service when you want it. Moderate.

... *NEAR CHICAGO*

Union Pier

PINE GARTH INN-
 www.pinegarth.com 15790 Lakeshore Rd. Union Pier. (888) 390-0909. There was a time when Union Pier was the place for families from Detroit or Chicago to go. Then it fell on hard times, but once again there is new and post-yuppie interest in creating wonderful spots to go. This one is adult oriented, peaceful, and perfect for a romantic getaway. Fresh flowers and

complimentary candy—champagne for special occasions. It is on the lake, with a private beach to hold hands on. Mention our book for a weekend discount. Inexpensive to moderate.

Utica

STARVED ROCK LODGE-
www.starvedrocklodge.com Starved Rock State Park 2668 E. 875th Rd. Oglesby Utica, IL. (800) 868-ROCK (7625). This is a rustic lodge in beautiful scenery about one and a half hours from Chicago. The pine-paneled lodge has some rooms with fireplaces, an indoor pool, and wonderful walks along the Illinois River. Inexpensive to moderate.

Mequon

SYBARIS-
www.sybaris.com 1024 Cedarburg Rd. Mequon, WI. (262) 242-8000. On a beautifully landscaped 10-acre site along the Milwaukee River, this country inn hideaway is part of the Sybaris chain that specializes in romantic getaways for married couples. Award-winning restaurant. Sybaris suites feature in-room swimming pools and whirlpool spas with extras like lots of mirrors. There are three other locations in the Chicago area. Inexpensive to expensive.

Dallas

ADOLPHUS HOTEL-
www.hoteladolphus.com 1321 Commerce Street.
(800) 221-9083. This hotel has an elegant English
atmosphere. The bedrooms have four-posters and are
tastefully decorated. For atmosphere, try the afternoon
tea. Moderate to expensive.

ROSEWOOD MANSION ON TURTLE CREEK-
www.rosewoodhotels.com 2821 Turtle Creek Blvd.
(214) 559-2100. This is the place to eat and sleep in
Dallas. All the amenities: marble baths, terry robes,
and more service than you will know what to do with.
There is an outdoor swimming pool and a health club.
Expensive.

Denver

LOWES GIORGIO HOTEL-
www.loewshotels.com 4150 East Mississippi Avenue. (800) 345-9172. This hotel has an Italian
theme; the public rooms make you feel as if you were
in a villa. The suites shine here, and the regular rooms
are not as special. A little bit away from downtown in
the Cherry Creek district— which helps you feel a bit
more away from it all. Moderate.

THE OXFORD HOTEL-
www.theoxfordhotel.com 1600 Seventeenth Street.
(800) 228-5838. This historic hotel features English
and French antiques, marble floors, and stained glass.
Located just off the Sixteenth Street Mall and Tabor
Center and within walking distance of Coors Field and

art galleries. Ask about their romance packages. Moderate to expensive.

HOLTZE EXECUTIVE VILLAGE HOTEL-
6380 S. Bonston St. Englewood. (888) 205-3315. Suites are in southeast Denver, near the Tech Center, offer a lot of privacy and include a comfortable living room and fully equipped kitchen. Complimentary breakfast and health club on-site with pool and fitness center. Some rooms have views of the Rocky Mountains. Inexpensive.

...NEAR DENVER

Boulder

HOTEL BOULDERADO-
www.boulderado.com 2115 13th Street. (800) 433-4344. Victorian elegance. 160 guest rooms and suites. Features magnificent views of Boulder and the Rocky Mountains. One block from award-winning pedestrian mall. Beautiful and bustling. Moderate.

Aspen

HOTEL LITTLE NELL-
www.thelittlenell.com 675 East Durant. (888) 843-6355. Want to splurge? Choose the Little Nell which has good rates off season. Pretty rooms—both right near the slopes (the Little Nell is practically on them) and in the middle of a wonderful walking town. If you want to stay downtown, try the Hotel Jerome, built in 1889, Aspen is out of our usual driving range—but, of course, worth it.

Vail

Visit *www.vail.com* Half the distance from Denver and a great village environment at Vail and at Beaver Creek. Both have nice examples of good chain hotels—the Sheraton, Westin, the Hyatt, etc.—and the scenery is scrumptious.

THE LODGE AND SPA AT CORDILLERA-*www.cordilleralodge.com* 2205 Cordillera Way Edwards, CO. (Vail Valley) (800) 877-3529. A really nice chateau-style lodge and spa. About twenty minutes from Vail in a beautiful setting with lots of privacy. All the rooms have lovely views of the mountains from their own balconies or terraces. Take your breaks at the health club, relaxing in the sauna or steam room or in an indoor heated lap pool. Choose from indoor and outdoor hot tubs. Moderate to expensive.

Colorado Springs

THE CHEYENNE CANON INN-*www.cheyennecanoninn.com* 2030 West Cheyenne, Co. Not far from Colorado Springs, with its fabulous Garden of the Gods and cliff-dwellings Native American ruins is this small, special bed and breakfast. You will feel far away because this l0,000 square feet mansion backs up to thousands of acres of wilderness. There are three especially commodious suites with king or queen size beds. Inexpensive.

THE ESTES PARK RESORT-

www.theestesparkresort.com 1700 Big
Thompson Ave. Estes Park (855) 377-3778 and
(970) 577-5400. The only hotel right on the
waterfront of majestic Lake Estes, this lodge just
came under new ownership and got a $2 million
renovation. It now features 54 spacious luxury
suites, with in-room spa treatments, plus indoor
pool, sauna, hot tub and fitness center. Its
Waterfront Grille restaurant has lakefront deck
and dining room with views of the 14,000 foot
high Long's Peak. Moderate.

ROMANTIC RIVER SONG INN-

www.romanticriversong.com 1766 Lower Broadview
Rd. (970) 586- 4666. All of the Inn rooms are terrific--
but you want the carriage house or the secluded
cottages. The river rushes by there. This place is
decorated for guys as well as women. The cottage beds
are cool, made out of birch or peeled logs, and the
Indian Paintbrush cottage is done with southwestern
Navajo artifacts (not to mention a swinging queen size
bed strategically situated in front of a fireplace). Other
rooms, and cottages also have romantic accoutrements-
such as fireplaces, beds-with canopies, and several
rooms have Jacuzzi tubs. The Meadow Bright cottage
even has a waterfall. Moderate to Expensive.

H AWAII

All the Hawaiian Islands have something to offer for an extended getaway-- here are some of our favorites:

Honolulu

KAHALA HOTEL AND RESORT-
www.kahalaresort.com 5000 Kahala Ave. (800) 367-2525. This elegant hotel is high on service and romance. They have a piece of land that goes out from their beach called "the kissing point" and why would you resist? Drive to Kailua, the long crescent beach now best known as the vacation spot for the Obamas; there are no hotels here, but it's open to the public and is probably the finest beaches to walk on the island. Moderate to expensive

ROYAL HAWAIIAN-
www.royal-hawaiian.com 2259 Kalakaua Ave. (800) 325-3589 Want to know you are in Hawaii and not Miami? Stay on Waikiki beach in this pink queen of Hawaiian hotels where tradition reigns. This is the beach ancient Hawaiian royalty preferred and a tasteful renovation of the 1927 hotel has kept it authentically and beautifully Hawaiian. It has a much celebrated restaurant, Azure, where you are always served fish caught that day. The rooms are traditional and romantic. Eating on the beach while watching the dancers or singers or participating in a luau just can't be topped. Moderate to Expensive.

Kauai

They don't call it the green island for nothing, you could get rainfall here. But it's the most lush, most

128

perfectly tropical and romantic of the islands. If you are a hiker, the Na Pali coast line is your dream hike (but be careful, this is for serious hikers only).

WESTIN PRINCEVILLE-
www.westinprinceville.com 3838 Wyllie Road, Princeville Hawaii. 808-827-8700. This hotel sits high on the bluffs overlooking the bay. All the hotels in Princeville have access to celebrated golf courses (the Prince Course has been called the best one in the islands by Golf Digest).

PLANTATION HALE SUITES-
www.plantation-hale.com 525 Aleka Loop, Kapaa, Kauai. (800) 775-4253. The Plantation is on the water but only a few units have ocean views. If that is important to you be very clear about it when you make your reservations. The units have kitchens, not fancy, but delightfully old fashioned. The Plantation's old home is now a wonderfully romantic restaurant, surrounded by spectacular gardens and tastefully lit up by small twinkling lights at night. Inexpensive to Moderate.

GRAND HYATT KAUAI RESORT & SPA-
www.kauai.hyatt.com 1571 Poipu Road, Koloa Hawaii. (808) 742-1234. If it's elegance you yearn for, this is a wonderful hotel with a gorgeous traditionally Hawaiian lobby. There are beautiful views to the water, elaborate pools, and romantic beach walks. You can have a massage next to the beach, enclosed in a small tent. The resort's restaurants are first rate and a wonderful place to have drinks and watch the sun go down is in their outdoor lobby bar. There are usually

high end local artisans selling their wares in the lobby
and everything is priced fairly. Expensive.

Maui

If you want beautiful beaches, fantastic golf courses,
whale watching in winter, and a fun town, Lahaina, to
visit at night, Maui is your island. A lot of the action is
along Kaanapali Beach.

SHERATON-
www.sheraton-maui.com 2605 Ka'anapali Parkway,
Lahaina, Maui. This hotel is at Black Rock at the end
of Ka'anapali beach where you can watch locals jump
or dive off into the water. The beach continues for a
long way and you can easily walk to the shopping
center where there are a number of good restaurants
and shops. Expensive.

THE WESTIN KA'ANAPALI OCEAN RESORT
VILLAS-
www.starwoodhotels.com 6 Kai Ala Drive. (808) 667-
3200 If you request the Villas, they have cooking
facilities inside and barbeques outside. Expensive in
high season, but moderate most other times of the year.

THE RITZ –CARLTON, KAPALUA-
www.ritzcarlton.com One Ritz-Carlton Drive. (808)
669-6200. This resort has wonderful areas to walk and
is surrounded by first rate golf courses. The Ritz ha
recreated the feeling of old Hawaii with a fantastic
general store that is a great place to have breakfast; its
private cove beach has a casual restaurant that serves
first rate food (and is open to

the public) to retreat to at water's edge when the sun or the waves tire you out. Expensive.

Houston

LA COLOMB D' OR-
www.lacolombedor.com. 3410 Montrose Blvd. (713) 469-4750. If you like the feeling of being pampered in your own mansion, come here. Only six rooms, each individually decorated with French themes. The nice part of this place is that they will cater to you, but they will also let you alone—perfect for our purposes. Elegant and expensive—but not over the top.

SOUTH SHORE HARBOR RESORT AND CONFERENCE CENTER-
www.sshr.com 2500 South Shore Blvd. (800) 442-5005. A nice getaway drive from Houston, just about halfway to Galveston. Right on the harbor, and most rooms have water views. The rooms are simple but nice. There is a fitness center, which has a lap pool and also a big Hawaii-type pool with a waterfall and a bar you can swim up to. There is also a boat center, and you can rent a sailboat or even go fishing. Moderate to expensive.

ANGEL ARBOR BED-AND BREAKFAST-
848 Heights Blvd. (713) 68-4654. Check it out on websites like Trip Advisor. This Victorian is on the National Historic Register, and it's a nice change of pace. There is a solarium, a gazebo, and those other Victoria's Secret romantic touches. Make sure you get one of the rooms with a private bath! Inexpensive.

HOTEL ZAZA-
www.hotelzazadallas.com 2332 Leonard Street. (800) 597-8399 This boutique hotel has several erotically charged theme rooms. In Dallas, we recommend the Out of Africa suite. Features romantic dining, and sexy art. The hotel's edgy atmosphere is sure to excite even the most erotic couples. Ask about their Romance Packages. Expensive.

Los Angeles

HOTEL BEL-AIR-
www.hotelbelair.com/los-angeles 701 Stone Canyon Road, Los Angeles (310) 472-1214.   Hidden away in the Bel-Air Estates, this is one of the most romantic hotels in the world. Newly remodeled, accommodations are more luxurious than ever. Celebrity Chef Wolfgang Puck just took over the hotel restaurant, as well as the terrace lounge in a stunning garden setting overlooking Swan Lake. Expensive.

HILTON CHECKERS HOTEL-
www.hiltoncheckers.com 535 South Grand Ave, downtown L.A. (213) 624-0000. Fully restored to its 1920s splendor, this is more like a boutique hotel than a Hilton. Perfectly located, just a block from Walt Disney Concert Hall and theaters, restaurants and nightlife. Ask for the Rose and Romance Package they created after being featured on "The Bachelorette"—roses, champagne, dinner, and room-service breakfast; be sure to see the stunning view from the rooftop deck. Moderate to Expensive.

SUNSET TOWER HOTEL-

www.sunsettowerhotel.com 8358 Sunset Boulevard, West Hollywood. (323) 654-7100. Wonderful skyline views from the pool and one-bedroom suites and great rooms, all with marble bathrooms and many with Jacuzzis. If you like art deco splendor and a trendy venue, this is the place to go. Expensive.

CHATEAU MARMONT-

www.chateaumarmont.com 8221 West Sunset Boulevard, West Hollywood. (323) 656-1010. Grab yourself a bit of history. There are 63 suites, but if you can, reserve one of those very private bungalows. There is a pool, fitness center, and lots of people-watching, since this is a place where Hollywood film people congregate. If you like "old Hollywood," this place will turn you on. Moderate to expensive.

THE CULVER HOTEL-

www.culverhotel.com 9400 Culver Boulevard, Culver City. (310) 558-9400. This historic art deco hotel is perfectly located. Very close to the beaches, but also close to Beverly Hills and Hollywood, this national landmark building (home to the Munchkins during filming of *Wizard of Oz*) is in the heart of the hippest part of Culver City. 46 rooms have been completely renovated, luxury bedding, art deco furniture and tubs. If you can afford it, request one of their suites, but if not, ask for their corner rooms. Nightly happy hour in their comfortable Lobby Lounge. Moderate.

THE INN AT PLAYA DEL REY-
www.innatplayadelrey.com 435 Culver Blvd., Playa
del Rey. (310) 574-1920. Right at the edge of a bird
sanctuary, and definitely designed for lovers. Lavish
breakfast, bikes to use on the 30-mile bike path that
goes along the ocean, and an outdoor Jacuzzi. Ask for
a queen- or king-size bed and a room with a whirlpool
bath and fireplace. Some have decks overlooking the
marina, and there are "romance suites" that feature
king-size canopy beds. Mention the book here.
Inexpensive to expensive (includes breakfast).

...NEAR LOS ANGELES

Catalina

HOTEL VISTA DEL MAR-
www.hotel-vistadelmar.com 417 Crescent Avenue,
Avalon. (310) 510-1452. This is a small, wonderful
hotel with 13 rooms and two suites. Some of the
rooms have hot tubs and fireplaces. We think the island
itself is romantic, and just going there can get your
blood racing. This hotel places you on the beach with a
view of pretty Avalon Bay. Inexpensive to expensive.

INN AT MOUNT ADA-
www.innonmtada.com 398 Wrigley Road, Avalon.
(800) 608-7669. If you are looking for something
really special, stay in the former home of the Wrigley
family. There are only a few rooms, so you have to
book way ahead, but you are really living the life of a
millionaire here. Expensive.

Laguna Beach

SURF AND SAND HOTEL-
www.surfandsandresort.com 1555 South Coast
Highway. (888) 869-7569. Perched over the sea, this
romantic spot makes you feel like you are on the
Mediterranean. Flowers everywhere, garden
walkways, and private patios. Moderate.

Malibu

MALIBU BEACH INN-
www.malibubeachinn.com 22878 Pacific Coast
Highway. (310) 456-6444. This is the perfect place
for a romantic interlude. It is right on the water, and all
the bedrooms have a full or partial view. There are tile
baths and fireplaces, and a cute lobby with tea or
coffee. Has just the right feel for a tryst. Moderate to
expensive.

Santa Monica

SHANGRI-LA HOTEL-
www.shangrila-hotel.com 1301 Ocean Avenue.
(877) 999-1301. Across the street from the Pacific
Ocean, this Steamship Deco small hotel offers a
romantic garden patio and two penthouse suites, each
with its own balcony. This boutique hotel has
undergone a unique multi-million dollar revamp. Each
sumptuous Shangri-La room and suite affords you an
iconic ocean view.

SHUTTERS ON THE BEACH-
www.shuttersonthebeach.com One Pico
Boulevard. (800) 334-9000. The regular rooms are
small, but the suites are nice and there are also a

pool, hot tub, and fitness center. The views are wonderful. We think this is a fun escape, right next to the boardwalk. Expensive.

Palm Springs and Other Desert Destinations

TWO BUNCH PALMS TRAIL-
www.twobunchpalms.com 67425 Two Bunch Palms Trail, Palm Desert Hot Springs. (877) 839-3609. The two of you can go here and pretend to be movie stars. There are hot tubs and rock and waterfall pools, and several other ways to pamper your body. We like it for the sexy places to relax or walk, and the privacy. Moderate to expensive.

LA MANCHA PRIVATE VILLAS AND SPA-
www.lamanchavillas.com 444 N. Avenida Caballeros, (800) 593-9321. This place offers both rooms and suites, but get the latter. There are two mineral pools, plus a regular pool and hot tub. Inexpensive to moderate.

TWENTY-NINE PALMS INN-
www.29palmsinn.com 73950 Inn Avenue, Twenty-Nine Palms. (760) 367-3503. An "in place" for LA escapees. Sixteen bungalows and smaller cabins. A pool, hot tub, and some pretty wonderful atmosphere. Inexpensive to moderate.

MARRIOTT DESERT SPRINGS RESORT & SPA-
 www.desertspringsresort.com 74855 Country Club Drive, Palm Desert. (800) 331-3112. This is a huge place—with three pools, several fine restaurants, champion golf courses, tennis, and

European spa. The rooms are very nice, and many of them open into suites with full kitchens. There is a dramatic lake and canals that some people love and others find too weird in the desert. Fabulous landscaping. Moderate to expensive.

Riverside

MISSION INN-
www.missioninn.com 3649 Mission Inn Avenue. Riverside (951) 784-0300. This is a large place (238 rooms), but it combines the Mission's historic heritage –it's a National Landmark -- with luxury and comfortable accommodations. They cater to romantic weekends and have some real bargains, such as combining a night in a suite with dinner, two massages, champagne, etc. There are beautiful grounds to walk, too. Moderate to expensive.

Santa Barbara

MONTECITO INN-
www.montecitoinn.com 1295 Coast Village Road. (800) 843-2017. Very close to Santa Barbara but known in its own right—and for good reason. This lovely place has charming suites and rooms. Many of the suites come with hot tubs, and the whole atmosphere is private and civilized. Moderate to expensive.

San Clemente

CASA TROPICANA-
www.casatropicana.com 610 Avenida Victoria, San Clemente, CA. (800) 492-1245. This reasonably

priced hotel is directly across the street from the main beach, and rates include a huge sumptuous breakfast served on the ocean-view patios. The penthouse (with large private deck and outdoor Jacuzzi) is best room. Note: This hotel features lots of stairs and no elevator. Inexpensive.

Ventura and Oxnard

THE PIERPONT INN-
www.pierpontinn.com 550 Sanjon Road, Ventura, CA. (805) 653-6144. A very lavish romantic destination, but cheaper than its equivalent in LA. A block from beaches and near bicycle paths, which would be nice to use on your break. Lovely views from most every room and best of all, there are very private cottages available as well as suites and rooms with fireplaces. There are spa treatments available, and the hotel does special romance weekends. Inexpensive to moderate.

INN ON THE BEACH-
www.innonthebeachventura.com 175 South Seaward Avenue, Ventura, CA. (805) 652-2000. Enjoy sunsets from your balcony. This is the only hotel in Ventura that is right on the sand. Not fancy, but a good value and great hideaway. Some rooms with fireplaces. Inexpensive.

Memphis

THE PEABODY-
www.peabodymemphis.com 149 Union Avenue, Memphis, TN. (800) PEABODY. If you're a serious music fan, there's a lot more than Graceland to pay

homage to in Memphis. Memphis has one of the great historic hotels in the country, the Peabody—a social hub since 1869. The Grand Lobby and the Peabody Athletic Club are Memphis institutions. The hotel's four-star rated Chez Philippe is consistently voted "city's best" by *Memphis* magazine. But the rooftop Skyway is a restored art deco restaurant that serves the best brunch in town, while the Plantation Roof offers panoramic views of the Mississippi Delta and hosts sunset serenades. Quirkiest of all, the legendary Peabody Ducks descend via elevator from their roof aerie every day at 11 a.m. by parading to the tunes of John Philip Sousa across a 50-foot red carpet that leads them into the lobby fountain, and reverse the ritual everyday at 5 p.m. (Don't believe us? Witness it for yourself on the Peabody web). Moderate

THE TALBOT HEIRS GUESTHOUSE-
www.talbothouse.com 99 S. Second Street Memphis, TN. (800) 955-3956. Each room is unique, ranging from 400 to 1000 square feet, and you can choose the one that suits your taste and pocketbook best by visiting the web site. Inexpensive to Moderate.

Miami Beach

THE KENT-
www.thekenthotel.com 1131 Collins. (866) 826-KENT. All the amenities for a song. Collins Avenue has been reclaimed and there is now a stylish scene—and the Kent 's sophisticated decor is part of this renaissance. Don't expect frills or luxury. Inexpensive.

THE TIDES-

www.kingandgrove.com 1220 Ocean Drive.
(800) 439-4095. This is a wonderful art deco
restoration. There are now 45 suites with 1930s style
and flair. A nice touch are blackout curtains for
sleeping in and a pool that accommodates topless
bathing. It is on the beach, with views from every room.
Moderate to very expensive.

THE ALBION, SOUTH BEACH-

www.rubellhotels.com. 1650 James Avenue. (877) 782-
3557. This beach hotel has a very nautical theme. There
are even six three-walled suites that are open to the
ocean. It's very high tech, with touches like
porthole windows that let you look into the pool. The
rooms are simple but airy. Moderate.

.... *NEAR MIAMI BEACH*

Boca Raton

THE BOCA RATON RESORT AND CLUB-

www.bocaresort.com 501 Camino Real. (888) 543-
1277. This is really a group of hotels, the "old
money" pink historic Cloister, the sleek Tower, and
the casual Beach Club—which is right on the water.
There is a shuttle that takes you from one to the other—
so if you stay at one you don't have to miss the others
entirely! We recommend staying at the older hotel and
visiting the beach by shuttle service—after all, you
won't be out of doors that much. Moderate with a few
expensive options.

Fort Lauderdale

THE RIVERSIDE HOTEL-
www.riversidehotel.com 620 East Las Olas
Boulevard. (800) 325-3280. This is the perfect
getaway find, overlooking the river and boats. The place
is "old Florida," but this is not a formal, elegant
getaway—rather, it is full of warm ambience for a
reasonable price. Mostly suites, inviting and casual.
Inexpensive to moderate.

Palm Beach

THE BREAKERS-
www.thebreakers.com One South County Road.
(888) 273-2537. This is the real thing. Italian
Renaissance splendor modeled on the Villa Medici in
Rome, this time on the ocean in an idyllic scene for romance. The rooms, we are assured, are soundproof.
Special romance packages. Expensive.

Minneapolis

NICOLET ISLAND INN-
www.nicolletislandinn.com 95 Merrian Street.
(612) 331-1800. This is a small renovated inn located
on a river island near the center of Minneapolis. The
rooms are cozy, decorated with antique furniture, and
the lobby is welcoming, with a fireplace and cozy
restaurant. For a break, consider the nearby park.
Inexpensive to moderate.

DOUBLETREE GUEST SUITES-
www.doubletree1.hilton.com 1101 LaSalle Avenue.
(800) 222-TREE. We are partial to suite hotels and
also, sometimes, some kitchen facilities. This one had a
wet bar and a room refrigerator and the usual amenities.
Not fancy, but nice, with a dignified lobby. Inexpensive
to moderate.

NEW ENGLAND

... IN CONNECTICUT

Mystic

THE INN AT MYSTIC-
www.innatmystic.com Three Williams Ave,
Mystic, CT. (800) 237-2415. This has all sorts of
accommodations; some are deluxe with balconies that
view the harbor, others are not so special. You have to
do a little investigative work to make sure you get
something really romantic, but after all, we have heard
that this is where Bogie and Lauren Bacall spent their
honeymoon. Moderate to expensive.

Norwalk

SILVERMINE TAVERN-
www.silverminetavern.com 194 Perry Avenue. (203)
847-4558. Small. In the middle of the countryside full
of charming antique shops. Several of the rooms have
fireplaces. There is a serious waterfall to listen to, and
it seems the perfect place to get away to for a lovely
weekend. It is popular, however (both the inn and the
restaurant), so reserve far in advance. Inexpensive to
moderate.

Kennebunkport

CAPTAIN LORD MANSION-
www.captainlord.com Six Pleasant St. (800) 522-3141. These lavishly decorated rooms have canopied beds and fireplaces—one deluxe suite even has a large multi-jet shower and a Jacuzzi-type bath. The town is bustling in the summer, but it's a wonderful, quiet escape out of season. Inexpensive to expensive.

THE INN AT HARBOR HEAD-
www.findbedandbreakfast.com 41 Pier Road. (207) 967-5564. This might be just what you are looking for—elegantly artistic furnishings and rooms with Jacuzzis, terry robes, and fireplaces, and all that right next to the waterfront. Moderate to expensive.

Lincolnville

THE INN AT SUNRISE POINT-
www.sunrisepoint.com 55 Sunrise Point Rd., Camden, ME. (207) 236-7716. This romantic location is near Camden. The very nice rooms are on the water—but even nicer, there are some very private cottages. Most of them have Jacuzzi bathtubs and fireplaces. Moderate to expensive.

... *IN NEW HAMPSHIRE*

ADAIR COUNTRY INN-
www.adairinn.com 80 Guider Lane,
Bethlehem, ME. (888) 444-2600. This is a 200-
acre estate originally designed by the famous Olmsted
Brothers, who also designed Central Park in New
York City. There is great service, lovely rooms, and
wonderful walks. Moderate to expensive.

BALSAMS GRAND RESORT HOTEL-
www.thebalsams.com 1000 Cold Spring Dr., Dixville
Notch, ME. (800) 255-0600. You might find this huge
place overwhelming, but it has every service you
could possibly want. It is nestled into the hills on the
water, and the vast acreage asks you to wander it.
Expensive.

... *IN VERMONT*

JACKSON HOUSE-
www.jacksonhouse.com 43 Senior Lane, Woodstock,
VT. (800) 448-1890. An elegant getaway with great
hospitality from the owners. Champagne and appetizers
are served in the beautiful garden during good weather.
There are both rooms and suites available. Moderate to
expensive.

THE INN AT SHELBURNE FARMS-
www.shelburnefarms.org 1611 Harbor Rd., Shelburne,
VT. (802) 985-8498. A striking mansion located on a
beautiful farm right at the edge of Lake Champlain.
Very romantic. Inexpensive to moderate depending on
the season.

HOUSE ON BAYOU ROAD-
www.houseonbayouroad.com 2275 Bayou Road, New Orleans, LA. (504) 945- 0992. For small and charming, this is tops. It was built in 1798 as a Creole indigo plantation, and still serves breakfasts that are fit for the plantation mistress and master. Rooms feature screened porches and poster feather beds, and some have oversized tubs and fireplaces, too. There is an outdoor pool and hot tub on its lush two acres of gardens and ponds. Inexpensive to Expensive.

SONIAT HOUSE-
www.soniathouse.com 1133 Chartres Street. (800) 544-8808. This is a truly romantic setting. There is a shaded courtyard lit with candles at night, vines trailing on balconies, and breakfast served in the courtyard. Bedrooms are located in several restored buildings, and the rooms vary from romantic to extraordinary. Moderate to expensive

MAISON DE VILLE AND AUDOBON COTTAGES-
727 Toulouse Street. (504) 561-5858. The hotel is very nice, but the real romantic retreats are in the cottages. The cottages are suites, and they have their own garden with a swimming pool in a shared central area. They are so romantic that a lot of other people want to book them, too—so reserve way ahead. There is also a romantic restaurant you probably want to reserve a spot in. Moderate.

WINDSOR COURT HOTEL-
www.windsorcourthotel.com 300 Gravier Street,
New Orleans, LA. (888) 596-0935. The exterior is
modern and not particularly alluring, but you enter
through a nice courtyard and the rooms are quite
appealing. They all have a sitting area, and most have
four-poster beds and traditional furnishings. There is
fastidious room service and very fine amenities
throughout. Expensive.

New York

THE INN AT IRVING PLACE-
www.innatirving.com 56 Irving Place. (800) 685-
1447. This hotel is in Gramercy Park a little bit off the
beaten path. It puts you firmly in nineteenth-century
New York. There are twelve guest rooms and suites
and many nice touches, like the ability to bring your
breakfast back to your room. No young children
allowed—which makes this perfect for a couple
getaway. Expensive by general standards, but not for
New York.

THE LOWELL-
www.lowellhotel.com 28 East Sixty-third Street.
(800) 221-4444. A historic hotel in a lovely, quiet
part of New York. Elegant decor, mostly suites, with
marble bathrooms, many with fireplaces and small
kitchens that are filled with romantic snacks like
champagne and cheese. The decorations are old
money: chintz, lovely prints, comforters, and antiques.
Great service and a romantic tearoom. Special place for
lovers. Expensive.

PARAMOUNT HOTEL-

www.nycparamount.com 235 West 46th Street. (877) 692-0803. If staying in the heart of Times Square sounds like fun, try this completely renovated boutique hotel. Reasonably priced with friendly helpful staff. Great bar. Ask about romance specials. Inexpensive.

THE PLAZA AT CENTRAL PARK SOUTH-

www.theplaza.com Fifty-ninth and Fifth Avenue. (888) 850-0909. Well, it's the Plaza! There is the wonderful Oak Room for dinner and the Plaza Court for Tea, the horse carriages outside, and the Park for your morning run. It's just about irresistible. The rooms vary a lot, though, so you have to be careful to get a large, cheerful one. Also, because the Plaza is now owned by the Westin, look for deals and special offerings. Expensive.

THE SOHO GRAND-

www.sohogrand.com 310 West Broadway. (212) 965-3000. A new hotel. High-tech with soaring spaces and an attempt to give a new and interesting hotel to the arts capital of New York. They have suc-ceeded in putting together both a chic and welcoming place with all the amenities and not too much sticker shock. Moderate to expensive.

... NEAR NEW YORK

The Adirondacks

THE SAGAMORE RESORT, LAKE GEORGE

www.thesagamore.com 110 Sagamore Resort Bolton Landing, NY. (866) 385-6221. Built in 1883 the Sagamore commands a stunning view of Lake

George. This lakefront resort offers luxury accommodation, excellent dinning, superb fitness and spa.

The Hamptons

HEDGES INN-
www.hedgesinn.com 74 James Lane, East Hampton. (631) 324-7101. A nineteenth-century house with all those nice New England touches. The rooms are all done with care—Laura Ashley prints and lovely linens. For our purposes, get one of the rooms with a fireplace so you can have a romantic candlelight dinner. Moderate to expensive.

1770 HOUSE EAST HAMPTON-
www.1770house.com 143 Main Street, East Hampton, NY. (631) 324-1770. A completely winning place with a great restaurant. Antiques everywhere, and each room has a personality all its own. Some of the rooms are extremely large and luxurious. Moderate to expensive.

Philadelphia

FOUR SEASONS HOTEL-
www.preview.fourseasons.com One Logan Square. (215) 963-9506. This is such a great chain—you can never really go wrong with one of their hotels. They are pricey, though, so look for special rate offerings. They all have an English-style elegance to them, fresh flowers, inventive menus, and usually very nice decoration, amenities, and bathrooms. They pride themselves on service. Expensive.

PARK HYATT AT THE BELLEVUE-
www.philadelphia.bellevue.hyatt.com 200 South
Broad Street. (215) 893-1234. Feel truly grand
walking in and out of this hotel with classic older-hotel
elegance. The rooms vary and can be small, but there
are very pretty ones (and decent noise protection).
There is a great health club. Very Philadelphia.
Expensive.

... NEAR PHILADELPHIA

Amish Country

WAYNEBROOK INN-
www.waynebrookinn.com 4690 Horseshoe Pike,
Honey Brook, PA. (610) 273-2444. The outside
of this hotel is eighteenth century, but the inside is all
new. There is an especially romantic dining room with
private nooks, perfect for making you feel as if you are
having an affair with each other. Bedrooms are nicely
decorated, and some have kitchenettes. Moderate.

Bethlehem

WYDNOR HALL-
http://mysite.verizon.net/wydnorhall/ 3612 Old
Philadelphia Pike. (800) 839-0020. Very nice, old-
city Georgian house. Elegant public rooms and
bedrooms. Wonderful breakfasts. Special attention to
details like lovely linens, heated towel racks, and terry-
cloth robes. Some suites include a two-person shower
that converts to a steam room. Inexpensive to
moderate.

Bucks County

MAPLEWOOD FARM BED-AND-BREAKFAST-
www.maplewoodfarm-bb.com 5090 Durham Road,
Gardenville, PA. (215) 766-0477. A beautiful
eighteenth-century stone farmhouse on a peaceful
five-acre farm. Charming bedrooms that include four-
poster beds or a two-story suite with beams and a
sitting room. Wonderful breakfast included. Moderate.

WYCOMBE INN-
1073 Mill Creek Road, Wycombe, PA. (215)
598-9600. This is a historic hotel that has been
remodeled with lovely, quite modern suites, most of
them with fireplaces and small kitchens. There is a
romantic restaurant and bar. Moderate.

STOCKTON INN-
www.stocktoninn.com 1 Main Street, Stockton,
NJ. (609) 397-1250. Technically not in Bucks
County, but this is right across the river from New
Hope—and what could be more Bucks County than
that? This is a pretty place with lovely rooms, some
with canopy beds, and suites. A romantic atmosphere
pervades this whole district. Inexpensive to moderate.

Poconos

COVE HAVEN RESORT-
www.covepoconoresorts.com 194 Lakeview Drive,
Lakeville, PA. (800) 432-9932. Tucked on the shores
of Lake Wallenpaupack, Cove Haven offers
tremendous variety among its 282 rooms. Besides
heart-shaped whirlpools and private pools, there are

theme rooms like the Champagne Towers (which features a 7 foot tall whirlpool in the shape of a champagne glass) and the Egyptian room features murals and a round king-size bed. The Roman Towers have 20 ft high ceilings with mirrors over the bed and twinkle sgtart bulbs. Rooms include Bose Wave Radio and other luxuries at an incredibly reasonable price. Inexpensive.

Phoenix

MARICOPA MANOR-
www.maricopamanor.com 15 West Pasadena Avenue. (800) 292-6403. This hotel has an enticing Spanish Mission-style architecture: stucco, arched doorways, and red tile. The place is on the formal and fancy side—lovely beds (some four-posters), fluffy feather beds, and fireplaces. There is a heated pool and hot tub. Lots of privacy—including a second building that has three suites and cottages on the grounds. Mornings begin with a breakfast basket delivered to each door. Moderate.

ARIZONA BILTMORE-
www.arizonabiltmore.com 2400 East Missouri Avenue. (800) 950-0086. Staying at this place is an experience. It is a masterpiece of architecture and is a mixture of desert and Mayan atmosphere. The great public spaces overshadow the rooms, but the grounds and general luxurious service of the place make up for it. Expensive, except off season in the summer.

THE BOULDERS-
www.theboulders.com 34631 North Tom Darlington
Drive, Carefree, AZ. (888) 579-2631. Want
perfect privacy for your romantic weekend? We
recommend this very pricey, very wonderful retreat.
They are all private "casitas" with southwestern style.
Beautiful big bathrooms (though some have only
showers!) and a lovely sitting area. All the amenities
(including wonderful salsa and chips) and great pools,
golf course, spa, and restaurants. Very expensive, but
there are times of the year when you can get a good
deal here.

… IN SEDONA

SOUTHWEST INN-
www.southwestinn.com 3250 State Route 89A,
Sedona, AZ. (800) 483-7422. One of the small luxury
(but affordable) hotels we recommend is near the 18th
fairway of the Eagle Mountain golf course. This is a
new boutique hotel with deluxe rooms and suites, each
with fireplaces, refrigerator, DVD player, two-person
whirlpool bath with plush robes, and complimentary
breakfast. Bathrooms in the suites have private
windows with a 50 mile Sonoran desert view.
Moderate.

L'AUBERGE-
www.lauberge.com 301 L'Auberge Lane, Sedona,
AZ. (800) 905-5745. Secluded cottages, fireplaces,
wrought-iron beds, some with canopies. Refrigerators in
rooms. Moderate to expensive.

ENCHANTMENT-

www.enchantmentresort.com 525 Boynton Canyon Road, Sedona, AZ. (800) 826-4180. Nestled in an exceptionally stunning canyon. Chic casitas, a perfect place for a getaway. Feel like one of the rich and famous. Tennis, swimming, hiking, riding, and romance. Excellent food. Expensive.

Portland

GOVERNOR HOTEL-

www.governorhotel.com 614 SW 11th Avenue. (800) 554-3456. This hotel's turn-of-the-century atmosphere sets the scene. The deluxe rooms feature sitting areas, high ceilings (some with skylights), and Jacuzzis. Some of the suites have fireplaces. It's definitely romantic. Expensive.

HOTEL VINTAGE PLAZA-
www.vintageplaza.com

422 Southwest Broadway. (800) 263-2305. This is one of those wonderful lobbies that set the mood. There are dark paneled walls, beautiful bouquets of fresh flowers, and an operating fireplace. Book one of the nine Starlight Rooms, which have beautiful views from very large picture windows. Luxurious linens and all the amenities. If you really want to splurge, there are town-house units with full kitchens, soaking tubs, living rooms, and loft bedrooms. Expensive.

The Coast

STEPHANIE INN-
www.stephanieinn.com 2740 South Pacific, Cannon
Beach, OR. (800) 633-3466. We couldn't resist this
one. It is perfect—right on Cannon Beach, a wide,
stunning, often windy expanse that is punctuated by
wonderful rock formations. Most, but not all, rooms
look out on the water. Each is romantically decorated,
and the public rooms are very inviting. You can also
stroll into town, which is absolutely charming—
though much better if you avoid the crowded summer
season. All the amenities: fireplaces, Jacuzzi tubs, and
some rooms with little decks or balconies. And guess
what—no small children allowed. Moderate.

CHANNEL HOUSE-
www.channelhouse.com 35 Ellingson Street, Depoe
Bay, OR. (800) 447-2140. This blue frame building
sets you right over the crashing surf; it is an
astoundingly romantic setting. Make sure you get one
with a great view and its own deck. Some also have
very private hot tubs. Inexpensive to expensive.

San Diego

THE U.S. GRANT HOTEL-
www.usgrant.net 326 Broadway, (619) 232-3121.
This landmark 1886 hotel has been totally redone and
now has some of its old grand manner back. It is right
in the heart of downtown and close to Horton Plaza
and the restaurant and theater quarter. Go higher up
and get a water view. Inexpensive to moderate.

THE HOTEL DEL CORONADO-
www.hoteldel.com 1500 Orange Ave. Coronado, CA.
(800) 468-3533. A true landmark on the National
Historic Register. Marilyn Monroe filmed "Some like
it Hot" here. The old architecture is wonderful and it's
right on the beach—but inside it is too often utilized
by conventions. Ask for a Romance Package in one
of the resort rooms with a water view in the newer
buildings. Excellent spa facilities. Expensive.

HORTON GRAND HOTEL-
www.hortongrand.com 311 Island Avenue, (800)
542-1886. Located in the Gaslamp Quarter, where
the restaurants, clubs, and theaters liven up the streets.
All the suites have fireplaces. Ask about romantic
packages. Moderate to expensive.

...NEAR SAN DIEGO

La Jolla

LA VALENCIA-
www.lavalencia.com 1132 Prospect Street. (800) 451-
0772. This is just what you would hope a getaway
hotel would be: small, charming, private, cozy, and
with a view of the ocean. Your room might be small, but
as long it has that ocean view, you won't mind. This is
such a pretty hotel. Moderate to expensive.

Rancho Santa Fe

INN AT RANCHO SANTA FE-
www.theinnatrsf.com 5951 Linea del Cielo.
(858) 756-1131. This is an incredibly lovely and
prosperous suburb of San Diego with an elegant, casual

feel. Most of the rooms have fireplaces and/or patios. There are tennis courts, a pool, six hot tubs, and some very inviting old California public rooms and restaurant. Moderate to expensive.

San Francisco

THE ARCHBISHOPS MANSION-
1000 Fulton Street. (415) 563-7872 An amazing place to stay. There are elegant appointments, and just grand public rooms. The majority of rooms have fireplaces, and quite a few are suites with their own sitting rooms. Each room is named Check out the photos on the familiar hotel and travel websites. You will find this place baronial, including the service and hospitality. Mention our book. Inexpensive to expensive.

THE HUNTINGTON, NOB HILL –
www.huntingtonhotel.com 1075 California Street. (800) 227-4683. This is the place to feel like an elegant San Francisco couple having a discreet affair while on a business mission. The hotel has a clubby, exclusive feel— especially by the romantic fireplace bar. There is fine service, even a free limo to the business district. Moderate to expensive.
... NEAR SAN FRANCISCO

Woodside

THE LODGE AT SKYLONDA-
www.skylondalodge.com 16350 Skyline Boulevard. (800) 851-2222. This log-and-stone lodge combines fitness with romance. Rooms have decks and soaking tubs, and there are endless hiking trails to try out. This

is a full-fledged spa that offers classes on New Age topics. A wonderful, healthy kitchen. Expensive.

The Coast

SEAL COVE INN-
www.sealcoveinn.com 221 Cypress Avenue, Moss Beach, CA. (800) 995-9987. A small country inn, with plenty of walking trails down to the beach or along the top for scenic vistas. Every room is a winner—with fireplaces and views of the gorgeous coastal water and cliffs. One of the most romantic landscapes in this world. Best of all, not expensive. Moderate.

PELICAN INN-
www.pelicaninn.com 10 Pacific Way, Muir Beach, CA. (415) 383-6000. The inn has a decidedly dressy English turn. Each room is very romantic; they all have canopy beds and lavish appointments. Moderate to expensive.

Mendocino

THE HARBOR HOUSE-
www.theharborhouseinn.com 5600 South Highway One Elk, CA. (800) 720-7474. Near charming Mendocino is Harbor House, a fabulous renovated 1916 craftsman style home, with six rooms in the main house and 4 private cottages with private decks and fireplaces. In addition to spectacular rock formations and ocean view, the property features magnificent gardens, secluded waterfalls, and steps that take you down to a private beach. If this doesn't sound enticing

enough, the room rate includes a four-course gourmet dinner. Moderate to Expensive.

Monterey

SPINDRIFT INN-
www.spindriftinn.com 652 Cannery Row. (800) 841-1879. You have a lovely view on the inns own beach, and inside you can feel snug in the always surprising Monterey weather. There are wood-burning fireplaces and big fluffy down comforters. There is also a wonderful wharf to walk—and that terrific aquarium, which is kind of romantic, too, if it isn't crowded. Moderate.

Pacific Grove

THE MARTINE INN-
www.martineinn.com 255 Ocean View Boulevard. (800) 852-5588. This is a wonderful getaway—less chic than Carmel and Monterey, but still lovely and much more reasonable than its more famous neighboring towns. The inn has wonderful Victorian rooms and nice suites with magnificent beds. There is a romantic view of the ocean from the breakfast room. Inexpensive to expensive.

Carmel

THE HIGHLANDS INN-
www.highlandsinn.hyatt.com 120 Highlands Drive. (831) 620-1234. This is a romantic place and a romantic hotel. Walking Carmel's shops and beaches is romantic—no matter what the weather. Many of the suites here have fireplaces and kitchens, and they are a

good value out of season. Not all the bedrooms have great views, but most of the public rooms do. Expensive.

... THE NAPA VALLEY

Many wonderful getaways here, among them:

Calistoga

FOOTHILL HOUSE-
Foothill Boulevard. (800) 942-6933 A lovely farmhouse with good food served and fine wine tasting in the afternoons (what a wonderful break that would be!). Lovers should ask for the private cottage. Regular rooms vary. We like the ones with four-poster beds and Jacuzzis. Evening cookies, sherry, or champagne. Mention our book. Moderate to expensive.

COTTAGE GROVE INN-
www.cottagegrove.com 1711 Lincoln Avenue. (800) 799-2284. These are simply wonderful cottages, each with a wicker rocking chair on its front porch, a fireplace, superior sound systems and VCRs, and soaking tubs. Too romantic for words. Moderate.

St. Helena

INN AT SOUTHBRIDGE-
www.innatsouthbridge.com 1020 Main Street. (800) 520-6800. New and lovely, right in the charming town of St. Helena. Has access to a very fancy spa at Meadowood, and another spa will be opening across the road. King-size beds, wood-burning fireplaces and tastefully decorated low-key rooms. Very

good Italian restaurant on premises. Wine tasting, horseback riding. Moderate to expensive.

THE ZINFANDEL INN-
www.zinfandelinn.com 800 Zinfandel Lane. (707) 963-3512. Since this area has some things in common with Provence, in the south of France, French themes predominate here. This is a chateau-like retreat, and each room has a spa tub, fireplace, and balcony. Inexpensive to expensive.

Yountville

THE CROSSROADS INN-
6380 Silverado Trail, Napa, CA. (707) 944-0650. This inn has only four rooms, but each is very romantic. The rooms are done up in a charming French provincial theme. You can have your breakfast delivered to your room, sip a glass of wine at night, and enjoy pastoral views from the deck. Moderate.

... SONOMA

SONOMA MISSION INN AND SPA-
www.fairmont.com/sonoma 100 Boyes Blvd. (866) 540-4499. This quintessential resort is known for its world-class spa, superb dining, and award-winning service. Surrounded by eight acres of eucalyptus-shaded grounds. The perfect romantic getaway located in the heart of wine country. Ask about special romance packages. Expensive.

THE KENWOOD INN AND SPA-

www.kenwoodinn.com 10400 Sonoma Highway Kenwood, CA. (800) 353-6966. This charming inn is a Conde Nast Readers' Choice Pick. Prices include gourmet breakfast and a bottle of Kenwood wine in your room. One of the best wine bars in the area. Day spa use is available to those who are not inn guests at a bargain facilities fee. Expensive.

Glenn Ellen

BELTANE RANCH-

www.beltaneranch.com 11775 Sonoma Highway. (707) 996-6501 This is a small inn on a big piece of property—1600 acres, to be exact. There are five very nice rooms and a great double-decker porch that has a swing and hammocks. Talk about relaxation and privacy. Your extremely nice price also includes breakfast. Moderate.

Seattle

FAIRMONT OLYMPIC HOTEL-

www.fairmont.com 411 University Street. (888) 363-5022. This is one of the elegant, great, old hotels, completely updated and well-run. There is a very nice health club and pool, and most rooms are nice. For a little more space, ask for a junior suite. The restaurants are romantic, and you are in a great location to walk downtown or to the waterfront. Ask about their special romantic weekends. Expensive.

THE INN AT THE MARKET-

www.innatthemarket.com 86 Pine Street. (800) 446-4484. This is a European-style hotel with a small flower-filled lobby, a great restaurant across the way, and a farmers market at your fingertips. Some of the suites are wonderful—and reasonable, for two floors, views of the sound and city, and French flowered rooms that are cheerful and comfortable. All rooms have access to the perfect rooftop garden that looks over Puget Sound and shipping lanes. Moderate.

THE ALEXIS-

www.alexishotel.com 1007 First Avenue. (888) 850-1155. This is a very tasteful hotel, with superb service. Some rooms have fireplaces. It is near the Pike Place Market and Pioneer Square. Small and service-oriented, they will cater to your every need. The rooms are decorated in Northwest subtle shades with flattering mellow colors. Very good restaurants. Expensive.

THE EDGEWATER HOTEL-

www.edgewaterhotel.com 2411 Alaskan Way Pier #67. (800) 624-0670. This is Seattle's only waterfront hotel. It has a wonderful lodge feel, all done with light pine so that the effect is light rather than dark. The theme carries through to the rooms—by all means insist on one on the water side. Great views in the lounge and restaurant as well. Moderate.

Snoqualmie

SALISH LODGE-
www.salishlodge.com 6501 Railroad Avenue SE.
(800) 2-SALISH. About one half hour from Seattle.
A personal favorite. This 1916 lodge got an award-
winning complete makeover. It sits above the
thundering 260-feet cliffs of Snoqualmie Falls in the
Cascades. The rooms are luxurious and spacious:
Each has down comforters, a hot tub, and a fireplace.
The dining room itself has private rooms over the falls
that are terribly romantic; sweethearts are discreetly
left alone. A good health club and a wonderful area for
hiking, biking, and fishing in the shadow of Mount Si.
Reasonable midweek; expensive on the weekends.

Whidbey Island

THE INN AT LANGLEY-
www.innatlangley.com 400 First Street, Langley,WA.
(360) 221-3033 Another favorite. This international-
style small hotel has all 24 rooms facing the water and
Saratoga Passage. Each room has a hot tub with an
unobstructed view and a fireplace. The rooms, like the
hotel, have a Northwest-Japanese peaceful feel—you
may never want to leave bed, even though the town and
the island have great restaurants and are worth
exploring. Moderate to expensive.

GUEST HOUSE LOG COTTAGES-
www.guesthouselogcottages.com 24371 State
Route 525, Greenbank, WA. (800) 997-3115. This
group of cottages are keyed to a honeymoon

atmosphere. They are lovely log cottages with pine paneling, skylights, private soaking tubs, kitchens, fireplaces, and big beds with down comforters. The kitchens are stocked with everything you need for breakfast the next morning. If this isn't enough for you, there is a larger log house for rent that is really spectacular. Everyone has access to an outdoor pool and hot tub. Moderate.

The San Juan Island

INN AT SWIFT'S BAY-
856 Port Stanley Road, Lopez Island, WA. (360) 468-3636. The inn itself is lovely- although intensely decorated near, not at, the beach, and perhaps too close quarters for our lovers. What you want here is their private cottage- separate from the inn- but you can go there for wonderful breakfasts and other parts of the island for wonderful lunches and dinners. The separate cottage is truly romantic- a view that gives you your own ocean, and a place to create the world's most romantic weekend. Total privacy. Moderate to expensive.

Tucson

ARIZONA INN-
www.arizonainn.com 2200 East Elm Street. (520) 325-1541. This is a private, quiet getaway. There are lovely grounds and fountains, an inviting pool, and the inclination to pay attention only to each other. There is a great lounge. Moderate.

WESTWARD LOOK RESORT-
www.westwardlook.com 245 East Ina Road. (800)
481-0636. This is a laid-back resort with three
pools, three spas, a fitness center, and a walking and
nature trail. The rooms are large and have either views
of the city or mountains, beamed ceilings, and wet bars
with a sitting area. There is a quiet charm to the
clustered southwestern buildings. You could be focused
on each other here. Moderate.

LODGE ON THE DESERT-
www.lodgeonthedesert.com 306 North Alvernon Way.
(877) 498-6776. This has a hacienda theme, and the
best places to stay are the adobe-style casitas with their
welcoming verandas. The rooms are spacious, and many
have wood-burning fireplaces. The place has a lot of
charm. Inexpensive to Moderate.

Washington, D.C.

THE MORRISON-CLARK HISTORIC INN-
www.morrisonclark.com 1015 L. St NW. (800) 332-
7898. This hotel is located in the middle of
Washington and has been placed on the national List
of Historic Places. There is a modern addition, and
rooms vary from small to luxurious; ones on the outside
facing the street are larger, with balconies. Ones on the
inner courtyard are smaller, but quieter. Ask for a room
with atmosphere: some have antiques and beds with
canopies. Inexpensive rooms and moderate suites.

THE WILLARD CONTINENTAL-
www.washington.intercontinental.com 1401
Pennsylvania Avenue NW. (202) 628-9100. A hotel
with a past. The lobby isn't too impressive, but you do

feel as if you are experiencing some piece of our country's history. There are some nice bars to hang out in. Most rooms are a good size and tastefully decorated. Moderate to expensive.

THE JEFFERSON-
www.jeffersondc.com 1200 16th Street, NW. (202) 448-2300. This is the hotel that will show you how visiting politicians (and politicians having affairs) live when they stay in a Washington hotel. This is restrained elegance. All the rooms have antiques or reproductions, and the bathrooms are large and lovely, as are the rooms. There is access to a health club and swimming pool. Rooms have CD players and VCRs— and everything else you need to feel like the Power People. Expensive.

... *NEAR WASHINGTON DC*

Virginia

Fairfax

THE BALIWICK INN-
www.washingtonhotels.com 4023 Chain Bridge Road. (703) 691-2266. Just a beautiful place, with some of the most handsome bedrooms you've ever seen. A fabulous food place, but the rooms are worth a visit on their own. They are impressive four-posters, hung with exquisite fabrics. Some of the rooms have Jacuzzis; all have lovely towels linens and amenities. This is a place that has many rooms perfect for lovers. Inexpensive to moderate.

Flint Hill

CALEDONIA FARM-
www.bnb1812.com 47 Dearing Road. (800) 262-1812. Just a little over an hour away from Washington, but light-years away emotionally. This nineteenth-century stone manor house is a historic landmark and is still a working cattle farm. There are lovely bedrooms with fireplaces and antiques, and amazing views of the Blue Ridge Mountains. There is also a very fine kitchen. Go for the one suite; otherwise, you might not get your own bathroom. This is a bit more rustic than most of the places we've mentioned, but it has romance written all over it. Inexpensive for the rooms, moderate for the suite. Inexpensive to moderate.

Middleburg

RED FOX INN-
www.redfox.com 2 East Washington Street. (800) 223-1728. This place absolutely reeks of hunt country ambience. Middleburg is a classy place, and staying here makes you feel as if you belong. The rooms aren't large, but they are charming. There is a wonderful tavern, a good restaurant, and some of the loveliest American countryside anywhere to explore for antiques or history. Moderate (and includes breakfast).

Williamsburg

LIBERTY ROSE BED-AND-BREAKFAST-
www.libertyrose.com 1025 Jamestown Road. (757) 871-3594. This establishment was made for romance: There are queen-size four-posters, fluffy duvets, claw-footed tubs, marble showers, and period fabrics. There

are also all those gadgets—like DVD players that we need for this weekend. Inexpensive for a room; moderate for one of the three suites.

Washington

THE INN AT LITTLE WASHINGTON-
www.theinnatlittlewashington.com Middle and Main Street. (540) 675-3800. This is rated as the best hotel in the South by many. People who are serious about food rave about the restaurant, and reservations are hard to come by. The twelve bedrooms are beautifully put together, with wonderful chintz patterns and comfortable furniture. There are DVD players and other amenities in the rooms. People come here to be treated well, and they are. Expensive.

White Post

L'AUBERGE PROVENCALE-
www.laubergeprovencale.com 13630 Lord Fairfax Hwy. (800) 638-1702. This is a place with the personal touch. The owners will tell you how to see everything in the area, and they are also intimately involved in the day-to-day-running of the place, including the kitchen. The food is wonderful and the rooms are all different, all charming. Ask about them: Some have canopy beds and fireplaces, or they might face the garden. Moderate.

Maryland

Annapolis

THE MARYLAND INN-
www.historicinnsofannapolis.com 58 State
Circle. (800) 847-8882. This is a wonderfully
shaped building in the center of town. The town is
close to D.C. and worth walking around in. The
colonial rooms are each unique, full of antiques, and
very comfortable. Good service and amenities. Moderate.

Middletown

STONE MANOR-
www.stonemanorcountryclub.com 5820 Carroll
Boyer Road. (301) 473-5454. Beautiful house on a
lovely piece of property. Views of fields, woods, and
ponds. Originally built in the eighteenth century, it has
had several additions and renovations. Very elegant
and very much organized around food—definitely for
serious gourmets. Still, the rooms are also wonderful.
There are five suites with queen-size four-poster and
other romantic beds. They also have Jacuzzi tubs
(sometimes for two) and vary with other nice
touches, such as sitting rooms, a special shower that
hits you with six jets, and a tub with underwater
lighting. Moderate to expensive (includes breakfast).

Oxford

ROBERT MORRIS INN-
www.robertmorrisinn.com 314 North Morris
Street. (410) 226-5111.There are several kinds of
accommodations grouped as the inn, including a lodge

and cottages. One of them is the Robert Morris Lodge on the Tred Avon River, and a room there with a view of the river would be just right. The rooms have a country motif, with claw-footed tubs in some of the rooms. Some rooms are more updated than others. The inn can send you a brochure to help you choose which room would suit you. Moderate.

CANADA

Montreal

RITZ-CARLTON, KEMPINSKI-
www.ritzmontreal.com 1228 Sherbrooke Street West. (800) 363-0366. We hate to nominate the obvious, but this is such a lovely hotel, we had to. Edwardian elegance; rooms are very pretty and many have fireplaces. The Ritz Garden is a very romantic place to have lunch during good weather. Health club privileges. Expensive.

HOTEL L'EAU A LA BOUCHE-
www.hotelspah2o.com 3003 Boulevard Sainte-Adèle, Sainte Adèle, Québec. (450) 229-2991. A member of the Relais and Chateau, it is an easy drive from Montreal. Wonderful French ambience; romantic rooms with fireplaces and terraces. Excellent dining. Moderate to expensive.

MANOIR HOVEY-
www.manoirhovey.com 575 Chemin Hovey, North Hatley, Quebec. (800) 661-2421. A member of the prestigious and almost always wonderful group of Relais and Chateau. On a lake, not too far a drive away. Beautiful sleigh and canopy beds, with wonderful

activities for every season. Gourmet food. Moderate to Expensive.

Toronto

PARK PLAZA HOTEL-
www.parktoronto.hyatt.com 4 Avenue Road, Toronto, Ontario. (416) 925-1234. Old World charm and one of the great romantic rooftop restaurants, with beautiful views of the city. Indoor pool and fitness center, with interesting neighborhood shops to look at during your break. Moderate to expensive.

ELORA MILL INN & SPA-
www.eloramill.com 77 Mill Street West, Elora, Ontario. (877) 242-6353. Astoundingly romantic 150-year-old mill inn placed over the dramatic falls of the Grand River. Recently renovated landmark. Antiques, quilts, fireside dining overlooking the falls. Rooms have vaulted ceilings, stone walls, fireplaces, and four-poster or brass beds. An hour's drive from Toronto. Moderate.

MILLCROFT INN-
www.vintage-hotels.com 55 John Street, Alton, Ontario. (888) 669-5566. Another find. Forty minutes from Toronto. Wonderful two-story cabins with fireplaces—outdoor hot tubs in some—and private decks. In a most beautiful setting—100 acres of woodland. Serious restaurant. Moderate.

WEDGEWOOD HOTEL-

www.wedgewoodhotel.com 845 Hornby Street, Vancouver, British Columbia. (800) 663-0666. Four Seasons may have better views (and is also a good choice in this city), but it's hard to beat this hotel for intimate European elegance. This feels like a private, personal hotel, and many of the rooms feel like small apartments because they have sitting rooms and fireplaces. Decks, too. 20% discount to our readers. Moderate to expensive.

LABURNUM COTTAGE-

www.bedandbreakfasts-bc.com 1388 Terrace Avenue, North Vancouver, BC. (604) 681-2889 About a half an hour from Vancouver, four rooms in the main house (with baths), and five cottages—all of which are absolutely charming. One cottage has a kitchen, fireplace, and skylights. Down comforters and all the right details, including gourmet breakfast delivered to your doorstep in the morning. Expensive to moderate.

RIVER RUN COTTAGES-

www.riverruncottages.com 4551 River Road West, Ladner, British Columbia. (604) 946-7778. Completely charming cottages and floating houseboats. Some with lofts, soaking tubs, kitchens, fireplaces, and water views. All have refrigerators and microwaves. Great respect for privacy. Breakfast delivered to your door. Special romance packages; mention our book. Moderate.

The Gulf Islands

HASTINGS HOUSE ON SALT SPRING ISLAND-
www.hastingshouse.com 160 Upper Ganges Road,
Salt Spring Island, British Columbia. (800) 661-9255.
This place is just too perfect. There are very different
kinds of wonderful accommodations, from rooms at the
main house to duplex separate buildings. All come with
their own down comforters and terry-cloth robes.
Some have wood-burning fireplaces and kitchenettes.
Most have stunning views of the sound. The main
house is a wonderful English residence that is used as
the dining room and for tea and sherry time. The food
is splendid and people are left alone—or spoken to—
as much as they want. Most of the herbs and vegetables
are grown on site. Expensive.

Victoria

ABIGAIL'S HOTEL-
www.abigailhotel.com 906 McClure Street,
Victoria, BC. (800) 561-6565. This rather large
bed-and-breakfast bends over backward to be
romantic. Fireplaces, comforters, and antique fur-
nishing and appointments. Very pretty throughout,
but each room is quite different, so ask. Moderate to
expensive.

LAUREL POINT INN-
www.laurelpoint.com 680 Montreal Street,
Victoria, BC. (800) 663-7667. Modern and large,
but don't let that fool you. The suites are affordable and
fabulous, with drop-dead views of Victrial Harbour.
Pitched beamed roofs, marble baths, spas in the
room—floor-to-ceiling windows to take it all in.
Expensive.

APPENDIX 6

A Few Favorite Foreign Places

Bermuda

Bermuda is a semitropical island a mere 568 miles east of the Carolinas, making it a short plane hop (under two hours) from virtually any East Coast city. The Gulf Stream gives it a remarkably mild climate— between 75 and 85 degrees in the summer—with no rainy season and practically guaranteed cool breezes. Bermuda epitomizes civilized living. This green and groomed island displays its ties and affection for its English ancestry. Bermudans drive on the left-hand side of the road, but you won't get a chance to try that yourself, as there are no rental cars on the islands. Tourists get around by some combination of motor scooter, ferry, taxi, buses, horse-drawn carriage, bikes, or walking.

A country of pastel houses awash with the tropical colors of Hibiscus trees, oleander and bougainvillea, Bermuda is perfect for the couple that wants a memorable getaway. In the summer, the island is quite crowded; the inexpensive off season is quieter and more romantic.

What to Do:

Golf: play the Ocean View Golf Course and hang around after the 18th hole for a dramatic sunset view of the North Shore.

Pack a picnic lunch for one of the many remote beaches that never have crowds (like Astwood Cove, tucked away in the steep cliffs in Warwick Parish) or head to West Whale Bay, which offers hillside tables overlooking a sandy cove.

Snorkel in sheltered bays (like Church Bay in Southampton) where the waters are calm and the marine life impressively varied.

Kayak around the island in wonderful quiet coves or take a romantic two-hour or all day sail.

Horse-drawn carriage ride through the quaint streets of Hamilton under the moonlight.

Where to Stay:

Cambridge Beaches
www.cambridgebeaches.com If money is no object, this is our favorite pick: a traditional setting and historic house greet you as you drive into a very private peninsula where every cottage is wonderfully decorated and has a marina or ocean view. It has two beach areas, one near the absolutely beautifully designed infinity pool and another that is long and isolated and where you may find just the two of you walking the pink sand (there's crushed coral mixed with the sand that give it coral hues). Its restaurant is excellent and looks out across the water. Favorite

175

dessert: their scrumptious nightly soufflé. Expensive in season; moderate off season.

Oxford House

www.oxfordhousebm.com If you have less money to spend, go for the Oxford House, one of the top Guest Houses (B&B) in Bermuda. There are 12 spacious rooms in this elegant townhouse, and the family that runs it gives first-rate personal service. It also offers the best location for Hamilton's restaurants, shops, and entertainment. Inexpensive.

Negril, Jamaica

"Everytin irie, mon." You'll hear this greeting all over Jamaica, but nowhere is it more true than in the serene beach town of Negril on the west tip of the island. The Urban Dictionary defines "irie" as being at total peace with your current state of being. The way you feel when you have no worries. Yes! If this appeals to you, we send you to one of our favorite beaches in the world—fine sugar-white sand extends far into the shallow pristine turquoise water (no pesky rocks under foot) –water that is not too warm, not at all cold. You can hang on a raft there for hours. Nearby reefs and crystal clarity make it a snorkeler's paradise. Jamaica is close to US, yet will transport you to total tranquility in an exotic foreign culture. If you love Bob Marley and the Wailers (their "Exodus" was named "Album of the Century" by *TIME* in 1999), you'll want at least one visit to his homeland. If you go in February, near Bob's birthday (Feb.6th), you'll hear tribute festivals playing his music all over the island.

Is it Safe?

You've no doubt read about the crime in Jamaica, but it rarely affects tourists as long as they use common sense. We strongly recommend that you avoid the city of Kingston and some sections of Montego Bay. We know people who go to laid-back Negril year after year and report they never felt threatened. We don't recommend you leave valuables on the beach while you go swimming, as petty theft is a problem, although every hotel has conspicuous security guards on duty, and uniform police patrol the beach at night. If this is a repellant image for you, then just go stay in one of the highly secure all-inclusive resorts where none of this is visible, or go to nearby Barbados instead. But if the local culture appeals to you, as it does to us, just go, use good judgment and enjoy yourself. One caveat: Jamaica is NOT a gay-friendly destination.

Getting There:

Fly into Montego Bay and rent a car for the real feeling of seeing Jamaica. Stop at the "Pork Pit" in Montego Bay for the best-tasting jerk chicken outside Boston Beach (home of "jerk" but way on the other side of the island). Take a leisurely drive to Negril; with the new toll road it's easy and is about an hour away. If you are less adventurous, just have the hotel arrange a cab to meet you at the airport and take taxis or tourist buses once you're in Negril.

Where to Stay:

Check into our home-away-from-home there, **Coco La Palm**. *www.cocolapalm.com* With its native architecture with open courtyards, lush gardens, this Minnesota family-owned small hotel sits right on the famous 7-mile beach. Unlike the cloistered big resorts, you will actually see and meet friendly Jamaicans on the beach, some strumming instruments to serenade you. Breakfast in its open-air restaurant starts you with fresh baked banana bread while you wait for your order. It's easy walking to restaurants and reggae clubs located nearby right on the beach. Inexpensive to Moderate.

If you prefer the seclusion and amenities (and extreme security) of an all-inclusive resort, see if there any special deals at **Couples-Swept Away**, a romantic couples-only resort. ***www.couples.com/swept-away/*** Given the generous no-cost inclusions (scuba and snorkeling excursions, sunset catamaran rides, free sightseeing excursions, water skiing and windsurfing instruction, unlimited golf greens fees), we rate this resort as "moderate" in price.

What to Do:

You can shop by just walking the 7-mile beach (and many vendors come to you while you're reading in your beach chair—ignore them and they will leave you alone, but it's also a great way to get your souvenirs with no effort whatsoever). Get a massage at the hotel after your morning swim.

Sunset at famous Rick's Café, the West End Cliffs being the perfect site to watch both the setting sun and cliff divers. You'll feel like part of the in-crowd as you listen to Rick's house band Dollyman jammin' true Jamaican Reggae. Great drinks. Try the banana daiquiris.

178

Golf at Negril Hills. Ask for our favorite caddy, Sharon Green.

Do a snorkel trip to the reef. Lots of boat owners will approach you on the beach and make you a good deal.

Day Trip to the Appleton Rum Factory. The Appleton Estate has been blending rums since 1749 and the Rum Distillery is situated beside the Black River in one of the most beautiful valleys in Jamaica, south of Montego Bay and Negril.

Day Trip to YS Falls. Near the Black River in Cornwall, Jamaica. About a two hour drive, including a quick stop at reggae pioneer Peter Tosh's Monument, just south of Negril.

Get a Tour Bus to Dunn's River Falls, and climb the terraced 600 feet high falls.

Where to Eat:

Get true local flavor by crossing the street at Coco La Palm and get to-go jerk chicken lunch at "Best in the West" then bring it back to the shaded beach tables at your hotel. The next day lunch in downtown Negril at "Juicy Patties." For ultimate romance, book a table for dinner at Xtabi on the Cliffs. The Rockhouse Restaurant also is romantic with great food.

MEXICO
Is it Safe?

Don't be scared away from all of Mexico from what you've been reading in the papers about the violence associated with the drug wars. They want your tourist dollars so there are excellent deals right now. If you do your homework, there are many places that haven't been touched by the violence, and you'll be safe. Our neighbor to the south still offers some wonderful, close vacation destinations in a warm and colorful foreign culture. Here are a few of our favorites:

- **Cancun, Isla Mujeres, and Playa del Carmen on the Yucatan Peninsula,**

We're not fond of the big hotel scene at Cancun, but we love this part of Mexico for its ancient culture and magnificent ruins, as well as the unusual Yucatan cuisine and hospitality. If you are a night reveler, then by all means stay in Cancun, consider staying at a place like Fiesta Americana at Coral Beach, and be right in the hub of shopping and clubs. Its 602 suites are all ocean front with private balconies, and it offers all amenities you want. But our true favorite there is "The Royal" hotel in Cancun (ranked #2 of 170 on Trip Advisor) -- it is an adult-only resort that has wonderful restaurants and service. Their motto is "Expect the Exceptional" and it fits – exceptional food, service, and accommodations! Among its many restaurants, we recommend Maria Marie for fine French-Mexican fusion.

A quick ferry ride takes you to Isla Mujeres, Island of Women, which has some quiet white sand beaches and romantic restaurants, many overlooking the turquoise waters and rocky coastline of the Caribbean. This spot is a special favorite of reef snorkelers. Without question, our favorite place to stay is **Villa La Bella** B&B, *www.villalabella.com* run by

Ashley and Curtis, American ex-patriots and hosts extraordinaire. Biggest Plus: Adults Only! No Phones! Unlike many B&B,s each of the six rooms circling the fresh water pool offers privacy, but we are partial to the large air conditioned honeymoon suite located upstairs in the main house that has skylights in the living/lounging area, a mini fridge, king size bed, large open shower, and two decks overlooking the sea. The sign outside announces "beer so cold it will make your teeth chatter" in the B&B's outside swing.

Where to Eat:

A short walk from Villa La Bella takes you past a bakery that will sell you the fresh goods they are making by night, and on to a baseball field, where you'll be able to eat on the sidewalk at "Beisbol Tacos"—some of the best you'll ever have—with huge fresh juice drinks. For a romantic restaurant, take a short cab ride into town and try any of these: The French Bistro right off Hidalgo, the main street in town, or El Varaderos's for authentic Cuban food or Manolo's for seafood and Mexican cuisine in a charming "Palapa" style restaurant.

What to Do:

There are lots of tourist buses from Cancun, but if you're staying in Isla Mujeres, host Ashley can arrange to have a personal driver pick you up at the ferry in Cancun and drive you via the toll road to the magnificent pre-Columbian Mayan ruins at Chichen Itza—get up early and your driver will beat the tourists' buses. You'll find it surreal to wander the enormous ruins practically by yourselves, with just the handful of tourists who stayed overnight in the small town there. Don't eat the tourist food; ask your driver to arrange a lunch at one of his favorite restaurants nearby and get an authentic slow-cooked stew called Cochinita Pibil or Vaporcito pork tamales.

If something in between the Cancun scene and serenity of Isla Mujeres is your speed, we recommend you head for Playa del Carmen. Set within an ecological park on the Mayan Riviera, **Xpu-Ha Palace** *http://www.xpuha-palace.com* hosts a natural wildlife reserve. They offer nearly 500 deluxe rooms in two-story, thatched roof bungalow style buildings, all with private balcony/terrace with hammocks, and oversize Jacuzzis.

If you prefer a much smaller hotel, with a staff that will literally plan your days for you, try the award-winning **Luna Blue Hotel** *www.lunabluehotel.com* with its 18 uniquely designed rooms set among a lush tranquil garden.

What to do near Playa del Carmen:

Swim with the whale sharks. Explore and swim in the Cenotes. And a trip to the Tulum ruins are a must—the only Mayan ruins right on the sea! They are different from all the other ruins. A must-stop en route back to Playa del Carmen is the Oscar & Lalo Restaurant *http://www.oscarandlalo.com* which serves great seafood and Yucatecan cuisine. It's about a mile down a dirt road from the highway, and you can kayak on the bay, lounge in hammocks, drink margaritas, and just hang out to relax.

Rancho La Puerta, Tecate

www.rancholapuerta.com   The price is all-inclusive of meals and classes; extra for spa treatments and private tennis coaching. Moderate to expensive, depending on specials and the amount of luxury you prefer in your "casita."

Other Things to Do:

Some of the great things to do there are taking a cooking class together (in an ultra beautiful building), taking a day off to go explore the budding Mexican wine industry a few hours away, taking a sculpture class together (novices do surprisingly well) and going to one of the smaller pools or hot tubs in the late afternoon or early evening when you are likely to have them all to yourselves.

- **San Miguel de Allende**

The best getaway for art lovers who would like to explore colonial Mexico is the completely charming San Miguel de Allende, central Mexico's oldest town. It seems completely invaded by American ex-pats and retirees who have come here for the good restaurants, interesting architecture including lovely colonial church spires, an innovative art scene, and great weather. There are great cafes where you can just sit and watch the people go by.

What To Do:

Art Galleries—go exploring along the cobblestone lanes. This is a town of artisans with good bargains that make great souvenirs of your time together here.

Sazon Cooking School. Take a class.

Horseback ride through the hills. There are several places but our favorite is Rancho Xotolar.

Nightlife—The town square really comes to life at night—it's the place to go to see people walking, talking, singing and sometimes performing.

Where to Stay:

Rosewood San Miguel de Allende
www.rosewoodhotels.com/en/sanmigueldeallende/
Affiliated with the Carlyle Hotel in New York City, this luxury boutique hotel has a spectacular view of the city. If money is no object, ask for the romance package and have an in-room Mexican dinner and couple massage, plus sparkling wine and roses. Expensive.

Casa de Sierra Nevada
http://casadesierranevada.com is a gorgeous small inn, very upscale, this is an Orient Express Hotel. Great amenities. 15 rooms in four Colonial Mansions. Expensive.

Casa Calderoni
www.casacalderoni.com This is one of the many cheaper but still picturesque inns that dot the town. Very helpful staff. On a quiet street in the heart of the historic colonial part of town. Found on many travel websites. Inexpensive.

- **Cabo San Lucas**

Actually, we like the entire 20 miles ocean corridor between Cabo San Lucas and San Jose del Cabo for its series of beautiful beaches and gorgeous places to stay, one right after the other. The water is turquoise and set against Los Arcos, an impressive rock formation and Lands End, the peninsula that marks the end of the land mass. This place, sometimes nick named "Arizona by the Sea," has its own special beauty. San Jose del Cabo is a more traditional small city with a quaint town square and more of an old world feel to it. Stay away during Spring Break when thousands of college students descend on the area, but know that it's wonderful when there isn't that kind of population inundation. If our choices are too pricey for you, don't worry, just go to your favorite travel websites and see hotels on the beach at every price point.

Where to Stay:

Villa La Estancia
www.cabolaestancia.com This is a private beach resort and spa, but you can rent their villas direct from owners or through websites like hotels.com or expedia. Expensive.

Pueblo Bonito Rose
www.pueblobonito.com This group has four oceanfront hotels in the Cabo area; some are adult only, which can't be beat for romance. Our favorite is the Rose. Moderate to Expensive, depending on room and season.

Barcelos Las Cabos
www.barceloloscabos.com If you prefer sleek international style, this all-suite hotel in San Jose del Cabo is close to the heart of town. Insofar as it's all inclusive, we rate this as moderately priced.

Cabo Surf Hotel
www.cabosurfhotel.com This 22-room boutique beach resort is located on one of the most privileged beaches in Los Cabos: Acapulquito. Moderate.

What To Do:

Nightlife in Cabo is legendary. **Nikki Beach**, the most famous club/lounge in Miami's South Beach, now has an outpost in Cabo with the same cool vibe, featuring tropical drinks with live music and guest dj's for dancing late into the night. This is a place to see "the beautiful people." On the other end of the spectrum is **Nowhere Bar**, a locals' hangout overlooking the marina. Great for sunset drinks.

Restaurants with Music include **Tropicana Inn**, modeled after colonial architecture, with nightly live traditional Mexican music and salsa dancing on Saturday nights; Deckman's in San Jose del Cabo features live blues, jazz, and blue grass.

Horseback riding on the beach with "La Playita" or try a longer ride at Costa Azul; they both take you through the San José Estuary where you will find out why this place has been declared a National Park and Bird Sanctuary.

Scuba Diving and Snorkeling to see the tropical fish in the exotic Santa Marìa Bay.

ATV Tours --there are wonderful dune parks directly overlooking the ocean.

Sport Fishing at Marlin Masters Sportfishing. Los Cabos is one of the sport fishing capitals of the world.

For more featured foreign destinations, please visit us:

www.thegreatsexweekend.com

and

www.hisandhervacations.com

ACKNOWLEDGMENTS

This book, like its previous edition, was created with the help of many people. An earlier version of this book was titled *The Great Sex Weekend: A 48-Hour Guide to Rekindling Sparks for Bold, Busy, or Bored Lovers* and was published in 1997 by G.P. Putnam's Sons in New York City. We again acknowledge our agent at the time, Elizabeth Ziemska, for giving us the initial idea. And we thank again everyone at Perigee Books, especially John Duff, the publisher, and Suzanne Bober, our editor, who gave the original version of this book the close attention that no one expects these days. And we thank Fran Rosen, too, for her excellent editorial contributions on the first edition. Cynthia Cobaugh helped to proofread and critiqued successive drafts.

And we thank everyone who helped us bring this edition completely up-to-date, and for travel ideas to greatly expand our getaway appendices. For their editorial research and artistic contributions for this 2012 edition of our getaway guide to great sex, we thank: Jessica J. Young and Ansley Pearce. We also thank Lisa Weinert for her suggestions on this edition.

For their original title suggestions, we thank Sandy Berry, River Malcolm, Renee Williams, Gail Zellman, Melissa Trikilis, and Frank Keshishian. Many people gave us advice that made a difference: Peter Adler, Ph.D., PattiAdler, Ph.D., Julie Brown, Angela Cohen, Debra D'Amato, Tom Darden, Ken Dorfman, Sean Dunn, Scott Grusky Debra Haffner, Lawrence K. Hong, Ph.D., Antoinette T. Hubenette, M.D., Marsha

Hunt, Kristen Hunt-Greco, Holly Lindsey, O. Lechuga, Monica Mendoza, Stewart Middler, M.D., Mike Neal, Barbara Nellis, Janelle Paige, Skip Paige, Brett Patton, Jennifer Powell, Candida Royalle, Joyce Santo-Diamond, Dean David L. Soltz, Robert Standen, Duane Tudahl, Monique Tu-dahl, Sandra Wade-Grusky, Ellen J. Wallach, and Milt Williams.

We again thank Good Vibrations and Tender Loving Things for allowing us to give samples of their products to our road-testers. And we greatly appreciate illustrator Malcolm Barter and his publisher, Prometheus, for allowing us to use his drawings from 77th *Complete Guide to Sexual Fulfillment* as inspiration for some of the illustrations which appear in this book.

Of course, every project is enabled by good friends and family going the distance. Jonathon and Nancy Goodson and Hugh Blake did us a great favor by giving us their lovely beach hideaways in which to write the earlier edition of this book.

Janet thanks PJ and Ed Hollister for respecting the priority of this project during a difficult family time, and for sharing their ideas for a perfect Negril vacation. Pepper thanks Cooper and Ryder Schwartz for their support. We both thank Cooper Schwartz for his invaluable assistance in the preparation of this book and our website.

Finally, we thank all of our road-testers—most of whom chose to remain anonymous—for taking the challenge and sharing details of their intimate experiences. It was their feedback and advice that made it possible for us to refine this program and make it as fun and rewarding as we hope it is.

Pepper Schwartz, Ph.D. and **Janet Lever, Ph.D**. coauthored the "Sex and Health" column for *Glamour* magazine for a decade. Both appear frequently in national media as experts in intimate relationships and sexuality. Both earned their Ph.D.'s at Yale University and are Professors of Sociology, at University of Washington and California State University, Los Angeles, respectively.

Dr. Pepper Schwartz has authored 17 books, including *Prime: Adventures and Advice on Sex, Love, and the Sensual Years*. She has been the Chief Relationship Expert for perfectmatch.com since it started helping daters meet online. Currently, she serves as AARP's Ambassador for Love and Relationship, writing an online column for aarp.org titled "The Naked Truth." She offers romantic travel advice on the nationally syndicated Peter Greenberg radio show. Dr. Schwartz is a past president of the Society for the Scientific Study of Sexualities and a charter member of the International Academy of Sex Research.

Dr. Janet Lever, after leading teams of researchers that designed the three largest magazine sex surveys ever tabulated, came to *ELLE* in 2002 to lead a series of annual surveys hosted on both the health and business sections of msnbc.com. *Her Office Sex and Romance Survey, Work, Sex, and Power Survey, "Good Sex" Survey, and Sex and Money Survey* are among the largest surveys on these understudied topics. Each of these internet surveys has been reanalyzed for social science, management, health, and medical journals.